All the Way

Also by Robert Schenkkan

The Great Society (forthcoming from Grove Press)

The Kentucky Cycle

By the Waters of Babylon

The Marriage of Miss Hollywood and King Neptune

Handler

Four One-Act Plays

The Dream Thief

Heaven on Earth

Final Passages

A Single Shard

The Devil and Daniel Webster

All the Way

ROBERT SCHENKKAN

Grove Press
New York

ISBN 978-0-8021-2344-2
eISBN 978-0-8021-9173-1

Printed in the United States of America
Published simultaneously in Canada

CAUTION: Professionals and amateurs are hereby warned that *All the Way* is subject to a royalty. It is fully protected under the copyright laws of the United States, Canada, United Kingdom, and all British Commonwealth countries, and all countries covered by the International Copyright Union, the Pan-American Copyright Convention, and the Universal Copyright Convention. All rights, including professional, amateur, motion picture, recitation, public reading, radio broadcasting, television, video or sound taping, all other forms of mechanical or electronic reproduction, such as information storage and retrieval systems and photocopying, and rights of translation into foreign languages, are strictly reserved.

Stock and amateur applications for permission to perform *All the Way* must be made in advance to Dramatists Play Service (440 Park Avenue South, New York, NY 10016, 212-683-8960) and by paying the requisite fee, whether the plays are presented for charity or gain and whether or not admission is charged. First Class and professional applications must be made in advance to William Morris Endeavor Entertainment, LLC, Attn: Derek Zasky (1325 Avenue of the Americas, New York, NY 10019, telephone: 212-586-5100) and by paying the requisite fee.

 All the Way was developed, in part, with assistance from The Orchard Project, a program of The Exchange (www.exchangenyc.org).

All the Way was the recipient of the 2012 Edward M. Kennedy Prize for Drama Inspired by American History, which is awarded through Columbia University.

Grove Press
an imprint of Grove/Atlantic, Inc.
154 West 14th Street
New York, NY 10011

Distributed by Publishers Group West

www.groveatlantic.com

14 15 16 17   10 9 8 7 6 5 4 3 2 1

To S. and J. Always.

INTRODUCTION

by Bryan Cranston

"We interrupt this program to bring you a special report."

I was seven years old, at home with a cold, when I first heard those words coming from the family's modest black-and-white television. It was a pretty afternoon in Southern California on November 22, 1963, but a dark cloud hung low over the nation. Walter Cronkite's authoritative image took over the screen and began to tell us in a disturbing, halting manner that our president had just been shot to death in Dallas, Texas. Cronkite wiped away a tear.

My mother shrieked in disbelief and immediately went to the ringing phone. The calls were frequent and each carried the same sense of dread: "I know, I can't believe it either, it's just awful." Each call was accompanied by copious tears. The entire neighborhood was in shock and great despair. Families gathered to share their grief. This was a horrible event on a scale that I had never experienced before. It scared me. I had never seen my mother so upset. My father too. Even at seven I realized something was much more important than my own existence, and I began to think that I should start to pay attention to other things, including who our president is and what he's saying to America. That focus fell onto our new leader, the thirty-sixth president of the United States, Lyndon Baines Johnson.

My impression of Johnson was that he was ultra-serious. He seemed like a lot of old guys of the era. The men in the gray flannel suits. Confident, laconic, powerful, and wearing what seemed like a perpetual scowl on his deeply creased face. A look of consternation. Of course, I didn't know it at the time, but years later I learned that my impression of Johnson was not correct at all.

Early in 2012, *Breaking Bad* gave notice. We would end production after shooting a final sixteen episodes by March of 2013. I was as proud as anyone can be of a body of work, but I was also satisfied with the decision because it would mean that we'd go out on our own terms. On top. It also meant that I should start looking for my next job, a compulsion inherent in most actors. I felt that after thirteen years on television (seven with *Malcolm in the Middle* and six with *Breaking Bad*) that a move away from the ubiquity of TV was my best option. I asked my team at United Talent Agency to look for a play and hoped that we'd find one that had a level of importance and gravitas that would be rewarding and worth the necessary devotion of time. They did their due diligence and came back with *All the Way*, by Robert Schenkkan. The title was derived from Johnson's campaign slogan in 1964, ALL THE WAY WITH LBJ! I had been offered a few plays that were destined for the Broadway stage before, but nothing like this.

All the Way had all the elements that any good story needs to keep the reader interested—better yet, invested—in the characters and plot. It's huge, it's historic, and indeed, important. The central role of the eclectic and unpredictable Lyndon Johnson was captivating. Like King Lear, he is a man both great in desire and accomplishments and weak in his despair and self-pity.

While doing research for the Broadway production, I came to understand him, to like him, feel sorry for him. He was an extremely complex man. He could be funny, threatening, warm, vindictive, sympathetic, and crude. Those who knew him speak of fascinating experiences with him—not always enjoyable, but always fascinating. Bill Moyers, the famous journalist, served as the president's press secretary from 1965 to 1967, and recently described him as "eleven of the most interesting people I've ever met."

Robert Schenkkan has masterfully crafted a play that tells the story of the first year of Johnson's presidency. It illustrates in compelling detail the difficulties of passing the landmark legislation of the Civil Rights Act of 1964 and Johnson's quest to shed the label of "accidental president" and win the office on his own merit in November of that same year.

Robert's play explores the inherent tension between Power and Morality by dramatizing Johnson's political acumen in getting things done by any means necessary. His well-known manipulation of the key players in Washington was even nicknamed the "Johnson Treatment," while other victims of the political arm-twisting aptly referred to it as receiving the old "Texas Twist."

But there are parts of Johnson's legacy that are more difficult to reckon with. He was the president who escalated the Vietnam War, a series of misguided decisions that haunted him and, I believe, informed the shocking and momentous decision he announced on March 31, 1968, not to seek a second term as president. The war had beaten him. In many ways he became a broken man. I suspect that the constant protests at the gates of the White House, the angry chants of "Hey, hey, LBJ, how many kids did you kill today?" tore a hole in his heart, maybe even literally. His cardiovascular system weakened to an irreversible point, and he succumbed to a third heart attack (eerily, just as he had predicted) in January 1973. Dying in the way he feared most . . . alone.

Yet despite his political downfall, Johnson's domestic accomplishments are legendary. No president in the twentieth century and beyond has had more success on the home front than he. Franklin D. Roosevelt comes to mind as the obvious contender to challenge that assertion, but he was in office before there were presidential term limits and served for nearly sixteen years until his death in 1944. Johnson himself invited the comparison to his idol Roosevelt, and even promoted the use of his own initials, LBJ, to echo FDR, one of the most famous presidents in American history.

Johnson was president for only five years, but his list of domestic accomplishments set down a foundation of laws that Americans depend on: the Voting Rights Act, Medicare and Medicaid, Head Start, the Corporation for Public Broadcasting, the National Endowment for the Arts, a strict environmental protection act, urban and rural development, his War on Poverty that helped millions of Americans rise above the poverty line, and the sweeping Immigration and Nationality Act, which removed all immigration origin quotas.

Even the Highway Beautification Act (a pet project of Lady Bird Johnson) gave the national highway system aesthetically pleasing scenery and landscaping to improve weary travelers' sense of well-being. But the shining star of legislation then, and now, was the historic Civil Rights Act of 1964.

This landmark bill is the centerpiece for the play. Signed by Johnson just six months after taking office, the bill banned racial discrimination in public facilities, interstate commerce, and employment. Protection for minorities was now enshrined in federal law. As history, and this play, illustrates, it was an extremely difficult battle, even within the warring factions of the "Negro movement" of the time.

Ideological differences among Democrats threatened to tear the party apart . . . and eventually, they did. After one hundred years of staunchly democratic rule throughout the South, Johnson's policies created a chasm between him and the powerful southern white men of power (dubbed the Dixiecrats) with whom he previously aligned himself, and indeed, the 1964 election turned the political tide in the South. As punishment for what it felt was a betrayal by Johnson, the South turned its back on him and the Democratic Party. It has been a Republican stronghold ever since.

Despite winning the election over conservative Republican Barry Goldwater by a landslide, Johnson fixated on the fact that he was the president that lost the South. It weighed on him, and he saw it as a rejection by his own people. He managed to get past that personal blow, went to work on developing his ambitious policies, and was the last of the truly liberal presidents. He believed that the purpose of the federal government was to create programs and protections for the people, backed by laws. He was once quoted, "What the hell is the point of bein' president if you can't do what you know is right?"

As an actor it is imperative to remain *subjective* to a character rather than *objective*. To justify instead of judge. It's very different preparing for a major historical figure such as President Johnson, from a fictional one like Walter White in *Breaking Bad*. Reams of source material are available and can become overwhelming. But there is another responsibility that comes with this territory. A responsibility to the real-life character and to the project itself. I learned that several years ago when I was preparing to play astronaut Buzz Aldrin in the HBO miniseries *From the Earth to the Moon*. In a very short period of time, I read so much about him that I lost mental clarity and found it difficult to bridge the gap between what was historically accurate and what was dramatically necessary for the good of the project. Lesson learned. While preparing for *All the Way*, I absorbed this gigantic character incrementally, relieving me of the pressure to capture exactly who the man was and allowing me to trust that his essence would eventually come to the surface and dovetail with the requirements of a theatrical production.

You never know what or when inspirational material will seep into your being that will inform the character you are incumbent to portray. One seemingly small moment at the Johnson Library in Austin, Texas, held such inspiration.

Making my way through the formidable exhibit on the Kennedy assassination, the Oswald shooting, and the funeral procession in Washington (who alive back then can forget the sight of little John John's salute?), I saw a small framed, handwritten letter addressed to the new president from Jackie Kennedy, dated less than a week after the assassination. In it Mrs. Kennedy describes two acts by Johnson that she greatly appreciated, one of courage, the other of kindness. The young widow expressed gratitude that President Johnson walked "with Jack" out in the open down Pennsylvania Avenue during the funeral procession. The Secret Service had implored the new president to follow in a covered vehicle for his protection. The full extent of the assassination wasn't clear. But Johnson refused. He and Lady Bird walked right behind the Kennedy family as a sign of respect for the fallen president. That courage resonated within me. As, to an even greater degree, did the next thing mentioned in the short letter. Mrs. Kennedy thanked the president for writing two letters to her children, Caroline and John, about their brave father. She also thanked Johnson for expressing the love and admiration he had for her late husband. This act by Johnson reverberated to my core and helped set the foundation of what I was going to create for my character. Ironically, it speaks to character itself. Cynics may argue that he did it out of his well-documented need for love and acceptance. Point taken, but regardless of the motive, this man, who just days earlier had ascended to the most powerful office in the country under dire circumstances, took the time to sit down and write to two small children about their father, a man whom they would never come to know. It is remarkable. Commendable. Compassionate to the nth degree. I feel that I am a compassionate person, but being honest with myself, if I were in his shoes I wouldn't have thought of such a selfless act of kindness. I don't think many of us would.

Most people in my generation have harbored contempt for our thirty-sixth president. But I have to admit that I have come to feel compassion for him. The failure of Vietnam is owned by President Johnson. There is no hiding behind that, nor should there be. His actions during that war contributed to countless loss of life. But as fair as it is to judge him on that failure, it is unfair not to include his collective achievements when assessing his legacy. It may sound as though I have become an apologist for Lyndon Johnson, and to a degree perhaps I have. He was an enormous figure in American politics. Johnson's political mold is broken. There may never be another politician like him. Who else would have the guts to risk losing his political base and lifelong friendships to pass sweeping changes in the law? Who else would beckon colleagues into the presidential bathroom and proceed to drop his drawers and take care of his business while not skipping a beat in the discussion? No, I think it's safe to say that we have seen the last of his kind, a giant among men in stature and determination. A dinosaur. Extinct but not forgotten.

The greatest value of any play on an audience is its ability to stimulate conversation. *All the Way* did just that during its Broadway run in 2014. Rejoice in the history, sentimentalize it, deplore it, regret it . . . but *talk* about it. I'm not suggesting we subject ourselves to revisionism, but as we recognize the Civil Rights Act (now past its fiftieth anniversary), it seems an appropriate time to *revisit* history and give proper acknowledgement to the accomplishments of President Lyndon Baines Johnson.

I hope you enjoy reading *All the Way* as much as I did.

Sincerely,
Bryan Cranston
2014

A NOTE FROM THE DIRECTOR

From the Playbill for the 2012 World Premiere

It's all Robert Schenkkan's fault.

Libby Appel first hired me as a guest director at Oregon Shakespeare Festival in 2002 to stage *Handler,* Robert's transcendent play about Pentecostal snake handlers. No one who saw it during its brief run can forget its power, and it is no overstatement to say that it changed my life. Without Robert's vision, I never would have fallen in love with this company, this community, and this audience. Three years later, I had the privilege of directing the world premiere of Robert's *By the Waters of Babylon,* written for long-term company members Armando Durán and Catherine Coulson. Three years later still, I was appointed OSF's artistic director. As Alison Carey and I began to build the first class of commissioned playwrights for our *American Revolutions: The United States History Cycle,* it was a no-brainer that Robert Schenkkan would be among them.

Robert's participation in *American Revolutions* was a foregone conclusion not only because of our personal history or his with this organization; Schenkkan has devoted his playwriting career to uncovering truths in American history. He won a Pulitzer for *The Kentucky Cycle,* but every Schenkkan play—no matter how intimate or epic the canvas—tells the story of how we aspire and how we often fail as a nation to meet up to our ideals.

All the Way chronicles the first eleven months of Lyndon Baines Johnson's presidency. The story tells how nation-shifting legislation was accomplished and how the presidency was won in 1964. As we approach our 2012 presidential election, its relevance is stunning. Robert's work, like so much of Shakespeare's, examines power and morality. To perform this world premiere in repertory with another *American Revolutions* premiere, *Party People,* set partly in the same decade, as well as Shakespeare's ultimate study of leadership in *Henry V,* reminds me of the deepest power of the Festival's dual commitment to classics and new work, side by side.

No matter when you are seeing this play during its run—as we head ever closer to Election Day on November 6—I trust that *All the Way* will take you deep into the period of its setting but also deep into the heart of who we are, and why we are who we are, as a nation today.

Bill Rauch
2012

All the Way

PRODUCTION CREDITS

All the Way was commissioned by the **Oregon Shakespeare Festival** for their American Revolutions: The United States History Cycle, a ten-year program of up to thirty-seven new plays about moments of change in United States History. It received its world premiere at the **Angus Bowmer Theatre** in Ashland, Oregon, on July 28, 2012. The production was directed by Bill Rauch. Christopher Acebo, Scenic Design; Deborah M. Dryden, Costume Design; Mark McCullough, Lighting Design; Shawn Sagady, Projections Design; Paul James Prendergast, Original Music & Sound Design; Tom Bryant, Dramaturgy; Rebecca Clark Carey, Voice & Text Director; U. Jonathan Toppo, Fight Director; D. Christian Bolender, Stage Manager; Mandy Younger, Assistant Stage Manager; Joy Dickson, Casting Consultant; Emily Sophia Knapp, Associate Director; Kristin Ellert, Assistant Video Designer; Monica Keaton, Production Assistant & Script Assistant. The production sponsors were The Chautauqua Guild, Charlotte Lin and Robert P. Porter, Edgerton Foundation New American Plays Award, The Paul G. Allen Family Foundation, The National Endowment for the Arts, The Harold and Mimi Steinberg Charitable Trust, The Kinsman Foundation. The cast was as follows:

President Lyndon Baines Johnson	Jack Willis
J. Edgar Hoover; Senator Robert Byrd	Richard Elmore
Sen. Hubert Humphrey;	
Sen. Strom Thurmond	Peter Frechette
Robert McNamara; Sen. James Eastland;	
Gov. Paul B. Johnson Jr.	Mark Murphey
Gov. George Wallace; Sen. Paul Douglas;	
Walter Reuther	Jonathan Haugen
Cartha "Deke" DeLoach;	
Rep. Howard "Judge" Smith;	
Sen. Everett Dirksen; Gov. Carl Sanders	David Kelly
Sen. Richard Russell; Jim Martin	Douglas Rowe
Walter Jenkins; Rep. William Colmer	Christopher Liam Moore
Stanley Levison; Seymore Trammell;	
Rev. Edwin King	Daniel T. Parker

Rev. Martin Luther King Jr.   Kenajuan Bentley
Rev. Ralph Abernathy   Tyrone Wilson
Roy Wilkins; MFDP Delegate   Derrick Lee Weeden
Bob Moses; David Dennis   Kevin Kenerly
James Harrison; Stokely Carmichael;
     James Chaney   Wayne T. Carr
Lady Bird Johnson; Katherine Graham   Terri McMahon
Secretary; Lurleen Wallace;
     Muriel Humphrey   Erica Sullivan
Coretta Scott King; Fannie Lou Hamer   Gina Daniels

All the Way had its New England premiere at the **American Repertory Theater**, Cambridge, Massachusetts, on September 13, 2013, and officially opened on September 19, 2013. Diane Paulus, Artistic Director; William Russo, Managing Director; Diane Borger, Producer. The production was directed by Bill Rauch. Christopher Acebo, Set Design; Deborah M. Dryden, Costume Design; Jane Cox, Lighting Design; Paul James Prendergast, Sound Design & Composition; Shawn Sagady, Projections; Tom Bryant, Dramaturgy; Rebecca Clark Carey, Dialect Coach. The cast was as follows:

President Lyndon Baines Johnson   Bryan Cranston
Lady Bird Johnson; Katherine Graham;
     Rep. Katharine St. George   Betsy Aidem
Walter Jenkins; Rep. William Colmer   Christopher Liam Moore
Secretary; Lurleen Wallace;
     Muriel Humphrey   Susannah Schulman
Sen. Hubert Humphrey;
     Sen. Strom Thurmond   Reed Birney
Sen. Richard Russell;
Rep. Emanuel Celler; Jim Martin   Dakin Matthews
J. Edgar Hoover; Senator Robert Byrd   Michael McKean
Robert McNamara; Sen. James Eastland;
     Rep. William Moore McCulloch;
     Gov. Paul B. Johnson Jr.   Arnie Burton
Rev. Martin Luther King Jr.   Brandon J. Dirden

Rev. Ralph Abernathy;	
White House Butler	J. Bernard Calloway
Stanley Levison; Rep. John McCormack;	
Seymore Trammell; Rev. Edwin King	Ethan Phillips
James Harrison; Stokely Carmichael	William Jackson Harper
Cartha "Deke" DeLoach;	
Rep. Howard "Judge" Smith;	
Sen. Everett Dirksen; Gov. Carl Sanders	Richard Poe
Coretta Scott King; Fannie Lou Hamer	Crystal A. Dickinson
Gov. George Wallace; Rep. James Corman;	
Joseph Alsop; Sen. Mike Mansfield;	
Walter Reuther	Dan Butler
Roy Wilkins; Shoeshiner; Aaron Henry	Peter Jay Fernandez
Bob Moses; David Dennis	Eric Lenox Abrams

All the Way received its New York City premiere at the **Neil Simon Theatre** on Broadway, with previews beginning on February 10 and opening on March 6, 2014. The production was directed by Bill Rauch and production credits are as above, except: Jane Cox, Lighting Design; Wendall K. Harrington, Projection Consultant; Paul Huntley, Hair & Wig Design; Peter Fitzgerald, Sound Consultant; Telsey & Company and William Cantler, CSA, Casting; William Farrell, Production Stage Manager; Hudson Theatrical Associates, Technical Supervision; Irene Gandy/ Alana Karpoff, Press Representative; AKA, Advertising; Alexandra Agosta, Company Manager; Richards/Climan, Inc., General Management. *All the Way* was originally produced on Broadway by Jeffrey Richards, Louise Gund, Jerry Frankel, Stephanie P. McClelland, Double Gemini Productions, Rebecca Gold, Scott M. Delman, Barbara H. Freitag, Harvey Weinstein, Gene Korf, William Berlind, Caiola Productions, Gutterman Chernoff, Jam Theatricals, Gabrielle Palitz, Cheryl Wiesenfeld, Will Trice. The Associate Producers were Rob Hinderliter & Dominick LaRuffa Kr., Michael Crea, PJ Miller. The cast was as follows (in order of speaking):

President Lyndon Baines Johnson	Bryan Cranston
Lady Bird Johnson; Katherine Graham;	
Rep. Katharine St. George	Betsy Aidem

Walter Jenkins; Rep. William Colmer Secretary; Lurleen Wallace;	Christopher Liam Moore
Muriel Humphrey;	
Sen. Maurine Neuberger	Erica Sullivan
Sen. Hubert Humphrey	Robert Petkoff
Sen. Richard Russell	John McMartin
J. Edgar Hoover; Senator Robert Byrd	Michael McKean
Robert McNamara; Sen. James Eastland;	
Rep. William Moore McCulloch;	
Gov. Paul B. Johnson Jr.	James Eckhouse
Rev. Martin Luther King Jr.	Brandon J. Dirden
Rev. Ralph Abernathy; Butler	J. Bernard Calloway
Stanley Levison; Rep. John McCormack;	
Seymore Trammell; Rev. Edwin King	Ethan Phillips
James Harrison; Stokely Carmichael	William Jackson Harper
Cartha "Deke" DeLoach;	
Rep. Howard "Judge" Smith;	
Sen. Everett Dirksen; Gov. Carl Sanders	Richard Poe
Coretta Scott King; Fannie Lou Hamer	Roslyn Ruff
Gov. George Wallace; Rep. James Corman;	
Joseph Alsop; Sen. Mike Mansfield;	
Walter Reuther	Rob Campbell
Roy Wilkins; Shoeshiner; Aaron Henry	Peter Jay Fernandez
Bob Moses; David Dennis	Eric Lenox Abrams
Rep. Emanuel Celler;	
White House Aide/Butler	Steve Vinovich
Sen. Strom Thurmond;	
White House Aide/Butler	Christopher Gurr
Sen. Karl Mundt;	
White House Aide/Butler	Bill Timoney

CHARACTERS

PRESIDENT LYNDON BAINES JOHNSON (LBJ)
Master politician. "Brave and brutal, compassionate and cruel, intelligent and insensitive, with an uncanny instinct for the jugular of his allies and adversaries." Possessing a marvelous, often crude sense of humor. Privately a font of extraordinary insecurity and vulnerability.

LADY BIRD JOHNSON
First Lady. An ideal political wife. Committed above all to her husband's political schedule and emotional needs. Tougher than she looks.

WALTER JENKINS
LBJ's loyal, long-suffering, and indispensable Chief of Staff. He has been with LBJ from the beginning; a kind of surrogate son.

SENATOR HUBERT HUMPHREY (D-MN)
Liberal leader in the Senate and a long-time champion of civil rights. Harbors White House aspirations.

MURIEL HUMPRHEY
Humphrey's wife and political confident.

KATHERINE GRAHAM
High-powered publisher of *Washington Post*. Alleged to have had an affair with LBJ.

ROBERT MCNAMARA
Secretary of Defense. Known for his rigorous intelligence, brilliant managerial skills, and acerbic manner. A chief architect of American policy in Vietnam

WALTER REUTHER
The tough, brilliant leader of The United Auto Workers (UAW) and an ardent ally of the Civil Rights Movement.

J. EDGAR HOOVER
FBI Director, whose paranoia and desire for power leads him to sanction massive corruption and illegal surveillance.

DEKE DELOACH
FBI. Hoover's right hand man.

CIVIL RIGHTS LEADERS

DR. MARTIN LUTHER KING JR. (MLK)
Founder and Head of the Southern Christian Leadership Committee (SCLC). Civil rights leader trying hard to keep the Movement together through impossible tradeoffs. Charismatic, insightful, and resilient.

CORETTA SCOTT KING
Married to MLK. Committed to him and to the Cause but troubled by the dangers he faces and the infidelities she suspects.

RALPH ABERNATHY
Reverend, civil rights leader, and best friend to MLK. Funny, compassionate, and devoted.

STANLEY LEVISON
White Jewish businessman and former Communist from New York. Chief advisor to MLK. A plain-spoken realist.

ROY WILKINS
Head of the National Association for the Advancement of Colored People (NAACP). Dapper, urbane, superior, he favors a conservative approach to civil rights advancement.

BOB MOSES
Brilliant civil rights strategist. Co-founder of the Student Non-Violent Coordinating Committee (SNCC). Known for his calming spiritual presence and total devotion to the Movement. Architect of Freedom Summer.

STOKELY CARMICHAEL
Brilliant, charismatic young civil rights field organizer. Bold and unimpressed by authority; a strong advocate for an increasingly more militant approach.

DAVID DENNIS
Young, passionate civil rights field organizer working in Freedom Summer.

FANNIE LOU HAMER
A former sharecropper turned civil rights leader. Co-leader of the Mississippi Freedom Democratic Party (MFDP). Uneducated, irrepressible, and inspiring.

JAMES HARRISON
Accountant for SCLC.

ANDREW GOODMAN
White college Freedom Summer volunteer, murdered in Mississippi.

MICHAEL SCHWERNER
White college Freedom Summer volunteer, murdered in Mississippi.

JAMES CHANEY
Local SNCC activist in Freedom Summer, murdered in Mississippi.

AARON HENRY
Co-leader of the Mississippi Freedom Democratic Party

THE DIXIECRATS

SENATOR RICHARD RUSSELL (D-GA)
The courtly but canny leader of the Dixiecrats, unalterably opposed to Integration. LBJ's political mentor.

REP "JUDGE" SMITH (D-VA)
A staunch segregationist and Chairman of the House Rules Committee.

SENATOR STROM THURMOND (D-SC)
Key member of the Southern Caucus. Known for his vitriolic racist language and extreme views on segregation.

SENATOR EASTLAND (D–MISS)
A plantation owner and virulent racist. Head of the Senate Judiciary Committee and leader of the "official" Mississippi delegation to the Democratic Convention.

GOVERNOR GEORGE WALLACE (D-ALA)
Racist Alabama governor. An outspoken, brash, and colorful political opportunist, and thorn in LBJ's side.

SEYMORE TRAMMEL
Officially a Wallace campaign aide but in reality his "bagman. "

LURLEEN WALLACE
Former Alabama Beauty Queen and devoted First Lady. Adores Wallace.

SENATOR BYRD (D-WVA)
Opposed to Integration.

REP. WILLIAM COLMER (D-MISS)
Opposed to Integration.

GOVERNOR JOHNSON (D-MS)
Opposed to Integration. Outspoken opponent of Mississippi Freedom Summer.

GOVERNOR SANDERS (D-GA)
Leader of the Georgia delegation to the Democratic Convention.

REPUBLICANS

SENATOR EVERETT DIRKSEN (R-ILL)
Senate Minority Leader from Illinois. An old colleague of LBJ's and a noted orator.

REP. BILL MCCULLOCH (R-OHIO)
Conservative Republican supporter of civil rights.

REP. KATHARINE ST. GEORGE (R-NY)
Liberal Republican supporter of civil rights.

DEMOCRATS

REPRESENTATIVE JOHN MCCORMACK (D-MA)
Speaker of the House. Liberal.

REP. EMANUEL CELLER (D-NY)
Liberal. Long-time supporter of civil rights.

REP. JAMES CORMAN (D-CA)
Liberal supporter of civil rights.

CS is a large oval playing area in the center of which is the President's desk. On three sides surrounding the oval are elevated "witness boxes"—curved seating areas much like a Jury Box where the Acting Company, the **WITNESSES**, *wait in full view of the audience until they enter the playing area. The Witnesses are not "in character" while they wait, but they are very much attentive to the action until they enter the scene. Witnesses may play several parts except for the actors playing* **LBJ** *and* **MLK**.

Far US Center is a bank of TV screens, one piled on top of the other. This is our electronic tally board (TB), as well as a screen for live images broadcast directly from the stage, archival newsreel footage, statistics, maps, super titles, etc. Scenes should move quickly, flowing one into another, never stopping to settle.

ACT ONE

In the half-light, the company enters and takes their place in the witness boxes. **LBJ** *moves DSC. The TB flickers to life with static like an old-fashioned black and white TV. The "Holding Pattern" appears—the famous American Indian Head. Then the countdown: TEN. NINE. EIGHT. SEVEN. SIX. FIVE. FOUR. THREE. TWO. ONE.*

Screen goes white. Fades to Titles:

NOVEMBER, 1963

SPOT ON on LBJ.

LBJ   I'm back in the Hill Country in the old days, hidin' down in the root cellar while a Comanche war party searches through the house just over my head, huntin' for me. It's so dark down there; like a grave. For this terrible moment, I wonder if I'm dead already, or buried alive. I piss myself like an idiot child crouchin' in the dirt knowing it's only a matter of time now before they find the trap door; discover me; haul me, screaming, up into the light where their knives gleam . . .

The Witnesses simultaneously strike the stage three times. With each strike, another image of President Kennedy's car entering Dealy Plaza appears on the TB. Last image fades out with SPOT on LBJ as . . .

LADY BIRD *gently shakes LBJ's shoulder.*

LADY BIRD JOHNSON   Lyndon? Wake up, honey. We're about to land in Washington.

Lady Bird stands on one side of LBJ as **WALTER JENKINS**, *his long-time aide, stands on the other. LBJ wipes the sleep off his face. They talk quietly; urgently.*

LBJ   You hear from Bobby?

13

WALTER JENKINS He'll be waiting on the tarmac. There'll be Reporters, too; you'll be expected to make a statement. Something short. Then we'll go straight to Blair House.

LBJ Reach out to the leadership as soon as we hit the ground; I wanta talk to each and every one of 'em. Today. *Now.*

WALTER JENKINS Yes, sir.

LBJ (*to Lady Bird*) You call Rose Kennedy?

LADY BIRD JOHNSON Yes.

LBJ Lord, what that woman's been through. Your lipstick.

LADY BIRD JOHNSON What?

LBJ Fix your lipstick. How did John Connally's surgery go?

LADY BIRD JOHNSON The doctors are optimistic.

LBJ Thank God for that. (*glancing about cautiously*) Jackie?

LADY BIRD JOHNSON Won't change her clothes. Says she "wants them to see what they have done to Jack."

LBJ See the way she stared at me when I was taking the oath?

LADY BIRD JOHNSON She's upset, honey . . .

LBJ We're all upset, Bird! (*quieter*) We're all upset. (*to Walter*) A televised address to both Houses of Congress as soon as it seems decent.

Sound of plane landing as LIGHTS widen. We are now in the Senate chamber. As LBJ moves past the **CONGRESSMEN**, *they each lower their heads and murmur respectfully . . .*

WITNESSES Mr. President. Mr. President. Mr. President.

LBJ stops. He is now addressing the Senate.

LBJ All I have I would have given gladly not to be standin' here today. The greatest leader of our time has been struck down by the

14

foulest deed of our time. No words are sad enough to express our sense of loss. John F. Kennedy told his countrymen that our national work would not be finished in the life of this administration, nor even perhaps in our lifetime. But," he said, "let us begin." Today, I would say to all my fellow Americans, let us continue.

Applause.

We have talked long enough in this country about civil rights. We have talked for one hundred years or more. It is time now to write the next chapter in the books of law. I urge you again, as I did in '57 and again in '60, *to enact a civil rights law so that we can move to eliminate from this Nation every trace of discrimination that is based upon race or color.*

The SENATORS and REPRESENTATIVES are surprised. They begin to applaud, the applause grows wild and cuts off abruptly as LIGHTS SHIFT. Oval Office.

In contrast to the subdued, dignified nature of his House speech, LBJ is loud, aggressive, and multi-tasking. As LBJ fields phone calls and questions his aides, his TAILOR measures him for a new suit.

TB board reads: **11 MONTHS TO THE PRESIDENTIAL ELECTION.**

SECRETARY   Senator Humphrey on One.

ADD SPOT on **SENATOR HUBERT HUMPHREY** *on phone. LBJ picks up phone.*

LBJ   Hubert! You hear what that nigra comedian, Dick Gregory, said about me? "When Lyndon Johnson finished his speech, twenty million Negroes *unpacked!*"

LBJ and Humphrey laugh.

SENATOR HUBERT HUMPHREY   It was a fine speech, Mr. President, dear to my heart, but I know some people are wondering, *did he really mean it?*

LBJ You can tell that Liberal crowd of yours, I'm gonna out-Roosevelt Roosevelt and out-Lincoln Lincoln! But they need to get behind me and back me up 'cause you know Dick Russell and the Dixiecrats are gonna fight me tooth and nail on this civil rights stuff. (*covering phone/to his Tailor*) Not too tight in the bunghole, there, Manny. And gimme some extra room in the pockets there for my stuff, my knife and my keys, and leave me some slack for my nutsack. WALTER, GET ME DICK RUSSELL! (*back on phone*) But time is *critical* here, Hubert, you understand me? All I want to get done, and the election only eleven months away . . .

SENATOR HUBERT HUMPHREY Well, if the Republicans are foolish enough to nominate Barry Goldwater, you'll beat him with both hands tied behind your back!

LBJ Goldwater's tougher than you think and I wouldn't count out Nixon but first, I have to win the Democratic nomination.

SENATOR HUBERT HUMPHREY Who else is there? George Wallace is a nobody . . .

LBJ A dangerous nobody, but it's not Wallace I'm thinkin' of.

SENATOR HUBERT HUMPHREY Bobby? You don't have to worry about Bobby.

LBJ Bobby Kennedy would just as soon cut my throat as smile at me.

LBJ's secretary enters.

SENATOR HUBERT HUMPHREY You know how strongly I feel about this civil rights bill, Mr. President . . .

WALTER JENKINS(*quietly*) Senator Russell on Two.

SENATOR HUBERT HUMPHREY . . . If there is *anything I can do* . . .

LBJ I'll keep it in mind, Hubert. We need to talk more about the bill. And the election! Give my love to Muriel . . .

SENATOR HUBERT HUMPHREY . . . I certainly will but I'd like to . . . .

LBJ punches the phone cutting Humphrey off. SPOT up on **SENATOR RICHARD RUSSELL**.

LBJ   Uncle Dick.

SENATOR RUSSELL   Mr. President.

LBJ   Lyndon. Lyndon, please.

SENATOR RUSSELL   No, Mr. President, it wouldn't be respectful.

LBJ   In public then, but nothing else changes between us. Hell, I owe everything I have to your good wisdom and generosity and don't you think for a second I'll ever forget it.

SENATOR RUSSELL   Well, you did throw me for a bit of a loop last night. State this country's in right now, a civil rights bill is about the last thing we need.

LBJ   Aw, hell, Dick, I got to throw Humphrey and the rest of those Liberals a little bit of red meat now and again.

SENATOR RUSSELL   For a hundred years the Democratic Party has had a lock on the South. It'd be a foolish thing to throw that away.

LBJ   Let me ask you something. You've finally got your heart's desire, *a Southern President*, after how long now?

SENATOR RUSSELL   Since 1849.

LBJ   A hundred and fourteen years! So, if you want to blow me outta the water, go ahead and do it but you will never see another one again. I say what I need to say when I need to say it but we're friends on the QT. Understand?

SENATOR RUSSELL   So this is election year politics?

LBJ   I'm an accidental President, Dick. I've got eleven months— eleven months 'til the election to establish myself as the man the people have *chosen* to hold this office. At the end of that time, would you rather have me in the White House talking about civil rights or Richard Milhouse Nixon?

17

SENATOR RUSSELL   Well, you, of course but . . .

LBJ   . . . There you go! I need you to hold the South for me, Uncle Dick. "Party Unity." It's gonna be critical. Lady Bird sends you her love and we'll expect to see you for dinner on Thursday as usual.

SENATOR RUSSELL   Oh, there's no need for that anymore, Mr. President . . .

LBJ   . . . Our Thursday dinners are sacred! Zephyr's making stuffed peppers. Bring your swimsuit and you can paddle your milk-white ass around the White House pool before dinner. See you then!

LBJ hangs up. SPOT on Russell out.

SECRETARY   Dr. Martin Luther King on 3.

LBJ angrily waves her away. To Walter.

LBJ   Where's the RSVP list to my . . .

Walter hands it to him.

WALTER JENKINS   . . . Congressional dinner party. They're *all* coming.

LBJ glances at list approvingly.

LBJ   Damn well better. And you best get yourself a good afternoon nap, Walter, so you can dance with all the fat women! (*calling out to Secretary*) Get me Katharine Graham at the *Washington Post*!

SECRETARY   J. Edgar Hoover on four.

LBJ punches #4 and picks up the phone. SPOT on **J. EDGAR HOOVER, DIRECTOR FBI**. *The Tailor brings in colored ties which LBJ inspects while he talks to Hoover.*

LBJ   Jay!

J. EDGAR HOOVER   Mr. President, the FBI is here to assist in any way we can.

LBJ   Aw, hell, Jay, you're more than the head of the Bureau—you're my brother! I have more confidence in your judgment than anybody else in town. If the Bureau needs anything from *me*, anything at all, you let me know.

J. EDGAR HOOVER   Well, in light of your announcement last night, we should have a discussion regarding Dr. King and company. I have recently acquired certain information which is deeply troubling . . .

LBJ "signals" Walter, who responds loudly, encouraging the Secretary and the Tailor to join him.

JENKINS/SECRETARY/TAILOR   Mr. President!/Mr. President?/Mr. President!

LBJ   Jay, I hate to interrupt but they're pullin' me six ways from Sunday. I'm very interested in this. We'll talk soon, I promise.

LBJ hangs up. SPOT out on Hoover.

Did King screw his sister or somethin'? That man is obsessed.

WALTER JENKINS (*quietly*)   I thought you were going to let Hoover go.

LBJ   Knew a good ole boy once, caught a rattlesnake bare-handed on a dare. Stood there with that big ole thing wrapped around his arm, head snapping this way and that, with this stupid look on his face, saying "Wow! It's a whole lot easier to catch one of these critters than it is to let it go!"

Secretary enters.

Don't know exactly what Hoover had on Jack Kennedy but he sure had his balls in his desk drawer. Bobby's too. (*to Secretary*) What? What?!

SECRETARY   Robert McNamara on Line 1.

WALTER JENKINS   He wants to resign.

LBJ punches phone #1. SPOT on **ROBERT MCNAMARA, SEC. OF DEFENSE**.

LBJ   Robert? So glad you called; you were on the top of my list!

ROBERT MCNAMARA   Thank you, Mr. President. I . . .

LBJ (*interrupting*)   I hope you're not even considering leaving the Cabinet right now. A man of your intelligence and knowledge is damn hard to replace; impossible! There's nobody else knows the Russians like you do, the Middle East, this mess in Southeast Asia.

ROBERT MCNAMARA   That's flattering, Mr. President, but surely you're going to want to bring in your own people . . .

LBJ   . . . You are my people. I'm keeping President Kennedy's entire Cabinet intact.

ROBERT MCNAMARA   I didn't know that, sir.

LBJ   I'm just an accidental President, Robert. Continuity is what the country needs right now while we heal. Can I count on you? Can the country count on you?

ROBERT MCNAMARA   Well, of course, Mr. President. I'd be honored.

LBJ   Good! Good. Five o'clock this afternoon, my office. We gotta lot of work to do.

LBJ hangs up just as . . .

SECRETARY   Katharine Graham on 2. And Doctor King is still on 3.

LBJ (*fierce*)   I don't need to be reminded of what I already know, Goddamnit! You're fired! Go on, get outta here! WALTER!

The Secretary runs out in tears. Walter runs back in.

Get me another secretary who knows what she's doin', and one with some meat on her bones, for Christ's sakes, not another one of these scrawny ole Washington bitties.

The Tailor begins holding up different shoes for LBJ's approval. LBJ picks up the phone and purrs.

Katharine.

SPOT on **KATHARINE GRAHAM**.

KATHARINE GRAHAM   Mr. President. What a wonderful speech!

LBJ   I hear that sweet voice of yours and I'd like to be like one of those young animals on my ranch—jump a fence. I want you to know I'd still be honored to speak to that Press Association of yours . . .

KATHARINE GRAHAM   . . . Well, that's terrific . . . !

LBJ covers the phone. To the Tailor . . .

LBJ   Christ, haven't you got anything there that doesn't make me look like a dago undertaker? (*back to Katharine on phone*) I gotta tough fight ahead of me, Katharine. Russell and the Southern bloc are gonna go after me hammer and tongs to keep this civil rights bill from even coming to the floor of the House. What I need is for the *Washington Post* to publicize as "racist" any member of Congress unwilling to give this bill a proper hearing. Can you do that for me, darlin'?

KATHARINE GRAHAM   I think we can manage that, Mr. President.

LBJ   You're the best.

Tailor exits. As LBJ finally picks up Line 3, SPOT comes up on **MARTIN LUTHER KING**.

I wanta thank you, Dr. King, for your public expression of support.

MLK   We were all very heartened by your speech last night, Mr. President.

LBJ   Well, it isn't going to be easy.

MLK   It's a difficult time, but . . .

21

LBJ ... It's just an impossible period. We're all still in mourning but somehow we've got to get a Budget out, an Agricultural Bill, and civil rights and the clock is ticking.

MLK As you suggested, the greatest tribute we can pay in memory of President Kennedy is to enact his civil rights bill, especially *Voting Rights*.

LBJ You're preachin' to the choir, Reverend! We're gonna pass that Bill "as is," without changing a single word, but it ain't gonna be easy. I'm going to have to have *your* help.

MLK Well, you know you have it, sir. Just feel free to call us for anything.

MLK Anything at all.

LBJ Thank you, Martin.

MLK (*CONT'D*) Regards to family.

LBJ Love to Coretta. Call me when you're up here next time and let's get together. And any suggestions you have?

MLK (*CONT'D*) Well, actually ...

LBJ ... Bring 'em in!

LBJ hangs up. LIGHTS down on LBJ. MLK hangs up. With him are his advisor, White businessman **STANLEY LEVISON**, *his closest friend,* **RALPH ABERNATHY**, *and SCLC Accountant,* **JAMES HARRISON**.

MLK He's just blowing smoke up my ass.

STANLEY LEVISON He came out on the Senate floor and called for a civil rights bill.

MLK Kennedy made promises, too, Stanley, but he never delivered. (*perfect mimicry*) "Not this year, Reverend. The, uh, the timing isn't quite right." Lyndon doesn't even have his charm.

RALPH ABERNATHY He's no George Wallace.

MLK Are you so sure? He's always been Senator Russell's Golden Boy—so deep in Russell's back pocket you'd have thought he was humping him. LBJ's maiden speech on the Senate floor was *against* an anti-lynching bill.

RALPH ABERNATHY (*wryly*) He was not *for* lynching, Martin; he was just against the anti-lynching *bill*.

STANLEY LEVISON He passed the '57 Civil Rights Act.

MLK After he gutted it first! Come on, Stanley, even Roy Wilkins cringed. Said that bill was like soup made from the bones of an emaciated chicken which had died of starvation!

STANLEY LEVISON Alright, he's a Southern politician who's spent his entire life trying to be President but he's there now. For the first time he can do whatever he wants.

MLK That's the question, isn't it? *What does Lyndon Johnson really want?*

STANLEY LEVISON Whatever it is, eleven months from now he has to run for re-election and he will damn sure need the Negro vote to win.

MLK Yes, but if we support him and he doesn't deliver, SCLC loses what's left of our credibility and the Movement could fall apart.

STANLEY LEVISON But if you don't support him . . .

RALPH ABERNATHY . . . we're out of the game before it even starts, and without pressure from us . . .

MLK . . . he might well decide to just service his Southern base. I know! I know! (*to Harrison*) James, let's hear your bad news.

JAMES HARRISON I've gone over the books very carefully and I think we can keep the doors open for probably another three months—if we let some people go.

RALPH ABERNATHY How is that possible?

JAMES HARRISON   Membership is dropping; contributions have dried up.

MLK   People are discouraged, Ralph, and I can't say as I blame'em. The Southern Christian Leadership Conference hasn't been providing much leadership. That's my fault.

RALPH ABERNATHY   Martin . . .

MLK   We've been standing still while we waited for Kennedy to honor his promises. (*to James*) Hold off on the layoffs as long as possible but cancel our charge cards immediately. (*to Stanley*) Any chance of another advance from my NY publisher?

STANLEY LEVISON   I'll ask.

RALPH ABERNATHY   We should cut SNCC loose.

MLK   We made a promise to Bob Moses.

RALPH ABERNATHY   Not that you'll ever get thanked for it.

MLK   At least the Students are getting things done. Can you scare me up some more speaking engagements?

RALPH ABERNATHY   Coretta's not gonna like that.

MLK   You think I do? Got to where I can recognize the airport I'm in just by the smell. (*a decision*) LBJ wants our support? OK. But *this President* is gonna have to deliver a real civil rights bill and we're gonna hold his feet to the fire until he does.

LIGHTS DOWN on scene, UP on FBI office. Edgar Hoover stands in the center, his ever-present #2, DEKE DELOACH, beside him.

J. EDGAR HOOVER   Play that middle part again.

Sounds of a tape recorder being rewound.

MLK (*on tape*)   Well, that's the question, isn't it? What does Lyndon Johnson really want?

STANLEY LEVISON (*on tape*)   Whatever it is, eleven months from now he has to run for re-election and he will damn sure need the Negro vote to win.

Hoover shoots Deloach a look of triumph.

J. EDGAR HOOVER   "Stanley Levison."

DEKE DELOACH   Yes, sir, Stanley Levison.

J. EDGAR HOOVER   Why is the so-called "Reverend" Martin Luther King taking advice from Stanley Levison, *a well-known Communist agitator?*

DEKE DELOACH   A very good question, sir.

J. EDGAR HOOVER   You're damn right it is.

Hoover considers.

(*thoughtfully*) Let's see who else King is meeting *outside* his office. I want *all his travel* covered from now on.

DEKE DELOACH   Legally-speaking, President Kennedy's wiretap authorization is no longer valid; we would have to go back to the Attorney General.

J. EDGAR HOOVER (*deep satisfaction*)   We don't need Bobby Kennedy's permission anymore. Who is that sanctimonious little prick going to complain to now? Lyndon hates his guts. Get it started.

Hoover starts off.

DEKE DELOACH   Yes, sir. Sir, our informant in Birmingham has relayed a report of a possible plot on King's life. What would you like us to do?

J. EDGAR HOOVER   Inform local authorities.

DEKE DELOACH   They may be involved to some extent.

J. EDGAR HOOVER   Inform. Local. Authorities.

LIGHTS UP on King house, Atlanta, MLK, suitcase in hand, and his wife, CORETTA. Strong current of tension between them.

CORETTA KING   You barely unpacked from the last trip.

MLK   I know.

CORETTA KING   The kids are starting to wonder who that stranger is.

MLK   Everything is up in the air right now, Coretta.

CORETTA KING   I know what this Bill means.

MLK   LBJ might be the Second Coming or just another Southern politician with alligator shoes and a salesman's smile. We got to keep the pressure on. *We got to get that Bill through the House.*

CORETTA KING   Well if you drop dead, I don't see how that helps things. *(looks off-stage)* Bunny, don't make me come in there! *(back to MLK)* You're going to wind up in the hospital again.

MLK   Staff has to be paid and money has to be raised. Who else is going to do that?

CORETTA KING   Not Ralph, that's for sure.

MLK *(ignoring the gibe)*   Did you pack my blue dress shirt?

CORETTA KING   Of course I packed your blue dress shirt. Let me come with you.

MLK   And who looks after the kids?

CORETTA KING   Oh, *now,* you're concerned about the kids.

MLK   That's not fair, baby.

CORETTA KING   I hate you being alone out there.

Abernathy enters abruptly.

ABERNATHY   Car's here.

CORETTA KING   I can help.

26

MLK kisses Coretta.

MLK   I gotta go.

LIGHTS DOWN on MLK/Coretta. LIGHTS UP on the Southern caucus and their leader, Senator Russell. A Private Club bar.

SENATOR STROM THURMOND   I will *leave* the goddamn Democratic Party before I will turn it over to a buncha Congolese savages!

SENATOR RUSSELL   Now, hold on a second, Strom.

SENATOR JIM EASTLAND   This Bill is just the thin edge of the wedge! You saw what they did in Birmingham. Integrated buses were just the beginning. Now you got to shop with 'em and eat with 'em and work with'em. We have been oppressed and degraded by black, slimy, unbearably stinkin' niggers!

SENATOR RUSSELL   *That's enough of that kind of talk!* That's exactly what they want to hear you say so they can dismiss us all as a bunch of redneck goons. We have to be very careful about how we handle this. In public, the issue is not about race, it is about the gravest possible assault on the United States Constitution which we are struggling to defend. Keep the issue framed that way in the Press and we win.

REP. JUDGE SMITH   The President's actively gatherin' signatures for a Discharge Petition to get the Bill outta my Committee in the House!

SENATOR RUSSELL   What do you expect him to do, Judge? He has to at least *look* lively on civil rights. When the time comes, he'll do the right thing.

SENATOR STROM THURMOND   He'll gut the bill?

SENATOR RUSSELL   He hasn't forgotten who his friends are.

REP. JUDGE SMITH   But if he gets the bill outta my Committee . . .

SENATOR RUSSELL . . . He still has to get it through the House and then he has to get it out of *Jim's* Committee, before it even comes to the Senate floor.

The men look at one another; it makes sense.

None of this should get in the way of *Party unity*. In this election we have a real chance to put a lock on both the House and the Senate and elect a Southern Democrat President. It's high time the South rejoined the rest of the country. We do our part and Lyndon will know who to thank come November Fourth. Don't worry about the President; I know how to handle him.

LIGHTS DOWN on Southern caucus. LIGHTS UP on **GOVERNOR GEORGE WALLACE***, his wife,* **LURLEEN***, and a large, enthusiastic crowd in Wisconsin. Simultaneously, Russell and LBJ watch Wallace on TV in the Oval Office.*

GOVERNOR GEORGE WALLACE   Lurleen and I are just tickled pink to be here in the Badger State for your Democratic Presidential primary. This situation we got up there in Washington with President Johnson reminds me of the little boy watchin' the blacksmith as he hammered a red-hot horseshoe. After he was done, the blacksmith splashed the horseshoe in a tub of water and threw it steamin' onto a sawdust pile. The little fellow picked up the horseshoe and then dropped it quick as a wink. "What's the matter, son, is that too hot to handle?" "No sir," the little boy said, "it just don't take me long to look at a horseshoe!" Well, it's not gonna take the people of this country long to look at this so-called "civil rights" bill and discard it just as quickly as the little boy tossed away that red-hot horseshoe.

Just yesterday, a fine-lookin' man grabbed my hand and said, "Governor, I've never been south of Milwaukee, but I am a Southerner!" Bein' a Southerner is no longer geographic, see. It's a philosophy, destined to be embraced by millions of Americans. It is the philosophy of the ordinary man, trying to do right by his family and his God, which says to the Federal Government, leave me the hell alone! If you want a *real* Democrat in the White House and not this messenger boy for Big Oil that we got by accident, then vote Governor George Wallace to be your Democratic nominee for President of *your* United States!

LBJ gestures and Walter "turns off" the TV.

SENATOR RUSSELL   He sure gets people stirred up.

LBJ   You and me have seen a dozen race-baiters come and go and they're all the same.

SENATOR RUSSELL   He took thirty-four percent of the vote in Wisconsin.

LBJ   A fluke.

SENATOR RUSSELL   He's runnin' a solid campaign in Indiana. A lot of our friends, yours and mine, like what he has to say.

LBJ   You talkin' about Strom Thurmond? I hear the good Senator from South Carolina's been making noises about switchin' parties and goin' Republican.

SENATOR RUSSELL   That's just Strom bein' Strom.

LBJ   When we get to Atlantic City, I will be the Democratic nominee.

SENATOR RUSSELL   But how damaged will you be?

LBJ   I'll be plenty strong enough for Goldwater in November.

SENATOR RUSSELL   What if Bobby smells blood in the water and decides to run at the last minute? You remember how those Kennedys did you three years ago.

LBJ   That little shit doesn't have his brother's balls.

SENATOR RUSSELL   He still has his daddy's money. You might win the nomination *but if the Party splits?* (*picks up civil rights bill*) All Wallace has got to beat you with is this damn civil rights bill and I don't for the life of me understand why you are givin' him this issue.

LBJ   At this point I'm more worried about the Liberals than I am about the Dixiecrats. We have to give them somethin' this time, Dick, you know that.

SENATOR RUSSELL   You have to *look* like you're giving them something. All I'm sayin' is, don't work quite so hard to get this Bill out of the House. If the Leadership over there can't do their job, that's no reflection on you, is it?

Russell offers the bill to LBJ. A moment. LBJ reluctantly takes the bill.

LBJ   I'll do what I can.

Before Russell can respond, Lady Bird enters.

LADY BIRD JOHNSON   Lyndon, you're gonna talk poor Uncle Dick to death, and here Zephyr's made him his favorite dinner and it's getting cold!

SENATOR RUSSELL   Saved by the belle! Bird, you look beautiful. As always.

LADY BIRD JOHNSON   And you're a terrible liar. As always.

SENATOR RUSSELL   The politician's curse . . .

Russell/Bird/Jenkins leave. SPOT on LBJ.

LBJ (*to the audience*)   "Any jackass can kick a barn down, but it takes a carpenter to build one." Sam Rayburn, bless his memory, said that to me the first time he invited me up to his office for one of his, "Board of Education" meetings. Bourbon, poker, and politics. I coulda kissed his bald head. God knows, I'd been kissing his ass since the day I moved to Washington, tryin' to get him to take notice of me, a dirt-poor Freshman Representative from bumfuck Texas, and when the call finally came, I felt like the Lord's Anointed. Sam Rayburn. *Speaker of the House.* Coulda had anything in the world and you know what Mr. Sam wanted, his greatest regret? "A tow-headed boy to take fishing." I heard that, and I did my damndest to be that boy. "Suck up." Uh-huh. "Brown noser." Sure. "Kiss ass." Yeah. I've heard it all. *Fuck. You.* Everybody

wants power; everybody. And if they say they don't, they're lyin'.
But everybody thinks it ought to be given out free of charge, like
Mardi Gras beads, 'specially to them, because, of course, they're
gonna do Good with it. Nothin' comes free. *Nothin'*. Not even
"Good." Especially not "Good." When the carpenter picks up his
saw, if wood could talk . . .

LBJ rips pages out of the bill.

. . . it would scream.

LIGHTS UP on Oval Office. Senator Hubert Humphrey enters in fury.

TB reads: **10 MONTHS TO THE ELECTION.**

SENATOR HUBERT HUMPHREY   You cannot cut the Voting Rights
section out of the civil rights bill!

LBJ   You can't pass a civil rights bill with Voting Rights intact. Not
this year. Not now.

SENATOR HUBERT HUMPHREY   It'll never even get out of the
House like this.

LBJ   The House is not the problem; the Senate is.

SENATOR HUBERT HUMPHREY   The House is a problem, Mr.
President. Hell, we can't even get it out of Judge Smith's Rules
Committee.

LBJ (*amused*)   You gotta give Judge Smith credit. I 'member how he
stalled the '57 Bill by claiming he had to go home to Virginia to take
a look at a barn of his that had burned down. Sam Rayburn said he
knew Judge Smith would do most anything to block a civil rights
bill but he never thought he'd resort to arson!

SENATOR HUBERT HUMPHREY   Have you made a deal with Smith?
Is that why you cut Voting Rights?

LBJ   I haven't made any kind of deal with the Judge.

31

SENATOR HUBERT HUMPHREY You told Dr. King that you wanted that Bill passed, "without one word changed."

LBJ When you go to sell a horse, you don't start by talking about it bein' blind in one eye and got the heaves.

SENATOR HUBERT HUMPHREY People are going to say that it's 1957 all over again and you're just gutting this bill!

LBJ Bullshit! It's still a damn good bill, Humphrey, and you know it. A great Bill! Real progress on Public Housing, Public Access, and School Desegregation. Don't you tell me that ain't nothin'.

SENATOR HUBERT HUMPHREY The Liberal wing of the Party will think you betrayed them.

LBJ Those are your people. It's your job to bring 'em around.

SENATOR HUBERT HUMPHREY My job?!

LBJ Don't be so modest, Hubert, you're the Great White Hope of Liberals everywhere.

SENATOR HUBERT HUMPHREY If I am anything like what you say, it's because people know I stand by my principles. I can't sell what I don't believe in! I won't.

LBJ This ain't about Principles, *it's about Votes*. That's the problem with you Liberals—you don't know how to fight. You wanta get something done in the *real* world, Hubert, you're gonna have to get your hands wet. You say you're the leader of the Liberal wing of the Democratic Party? Then show me some goddamn leadership!

Beat

These three good ole boys were talkin' about the "ugliest sound in the world." The first one said, "I once slipped in the lumber yard and fell onto the belt that fed the buzz saw. As it was dragging me closer I could hear that saw whining and I mean to tell you, that was the ugliest sound in the world." The second boy says, "Ah, hell, that ain't nothing. I once was so drunk I fell onto the railroad track and got my leg all twisted up under one of them ties just as a big ole freight train was bearing down. I lay there as that train came towards me—chugachug, chugachug, chugachug—and *that* is the ugliest sound in the world." The third boy says, "You fellas don't know shit. I was once screwin' this purty gal when all of a sudden her husband come home? I jumped buck naked out the window but he grabbed my balls with one hand and pulled out his big ole jack knife with the other, and set to opening the blade with his mouth. And the click, click, click of his teeth on that blade, that was the ugliest sound in the world!"

You know what the ugliest sound in the world is, Hubert? The tick, tick, tick of a clock. All the men in my family die young—I nearly died of that heart attack ten years ago.

SENATOR HUBERT HUMPHREY A terrible time.

LBJ I ain't got much time left. And you and me, we only got until the convention in August, while people are still grieving Kennedy's death, to get this Bill passed. If we don't act now, this opportunity to do something about civil rights will disappear forever. Are you in, or are you out?

A moment.

SENATOR HUBERT HUMPHREY Can you get the bill out of the House Rules Committee?

LBJ Leave Judge Smith to me.

SENATOR HUBERT HUMPHREY Without anymore compromises?

LBJ Yes.

SENATOR HUBERT HUMPHREY And voting rights?

LBJ Next year. You have my word.

SENATOR HUBERT HUMPHREY This is going to be a very difficult sell, Mr. President.

LBJ That's why I want you to be the Floor Manager of this bill.

SENATOR HUBERT HUMPHREY (*surprised and flattered*)   Floor Manager? I assumed the Senate Majority Leader . . .

LBJ   . . . Mike's a good man but I need someone more personable. People like you, Hubert. Hell, even Dick Russell likes you. You know I'm under a lot of pressure to announce my running mate for the election. Some people tell me I ought to pick Bobby Kennedy but I'm not so sure of his loyalty. There was a time, not so long ago, when him and the rest of his Harvard Blue Bloods looked down their noses at me like I was some kind of country bumpkin.

SENATOR HUBERT HUMPHREY   I'm sure that's not the . . .

LBJ   . . . They treated me like dog shit! All of 'em. Jackie called me a "cowboy oaf." Now, you show me that you have the guts to push this thing through, all the way, and you make yourself a very real candidate to be my Vice President. Of the United States. Of America. A step away from the White House. And as we've seen, anything can happen from there.

SENATOR HUBERT HUMPHREY   I'll do everything I can, Mr. President.

LBJ   Well, go on then, get started! What're you doin' standin' here!

LIGHTS DOWN on LBJ. Humphrey remains in a SPOT taking off his coat and tie as his wife, **MURIEL***, joins him.*

SENATOR HUBERT HUMPHREY   The question is, did I hear him say what I thought I heard him say? Or did I hear him say what he knows I want to hear him say?

MURIEL HUMPHREY   What did he say?

SENATOR HUBERT HUMPHREY   He offered me the VP slot.

Muriel throws her arms around him.

MURIEL HUMPHREY   Oh, my God, that's wonderful!

SENATOR HUBERT HUMPHREY   I know, I know! Well, *conditionally*.

MURIEL HUMPHREY What does that mean?

SENATOR HUBERT HUMPHREY It means I'm the front runner
but he's going to extract his pound of flesh first—which is alright,
I guess, depending on where he's cutting it from. (*more seriously*) I
don't think I can ever get elected President on my own, Muriel. I
don't have Bobby's money or LBJ's oil and gas friends. The only way
I'll ever get to the White House is through the Vice-Presidency.

MURIEL HUMPHREY What do your advisors say?

SENATOR HUBERT HUMPHREY If I tie myself too close to Lyndon
I'll lose my freedom but—I'm more worried about compromising myself.

A moment

What does my chief advisor think?

MURIEL HUMPHREY Does he really support the Bill?

SENATOR HUBERT HUMPHREY With Lyndon you never know
but even if he means just half of what he says, we could change this
Country forever.

MURIEL HUMPHREY (*softly*) And you could be President.

*Muriel kisses Humphrey as LIGHTS DOWN. UP on MLK/LBJ in
the Oval Office. A **BUTLER** brings out a silver coffee set. LBJ pours for
both men.*

MLK My people are *deeply* concerned, Mr. President.

LBJ I understand.

MLK You promised the country a civil rights bill and the Voting
Rights component is critical . . .

LBJ . . . Absolutely critical, and we're gonna fix that, just not in
this Bill. Right now, we're gonna take care of segregation in Public
Accommodations first. Do you know every year my cook, Zephyr
Wright, best chicken-fried steak you ever put in your mouth, well,
every year, she and her husband drive my Packard from Washington

35

back down to the Ranch for me. Now Zephyr's college educated and all, but she can't use any restrooms on any of those highways 'cause they're all "whites only." She's got to squat in a field by the side of the road to pee like a dog! Now, that's just not right, and by God, we're gonna fix that.

MLK (*pointedly*)   The Civil Right Bill of 1957 was supposed to fix that.

As LBJ puts several teaspoons of sugar in his own tea . . .

LBJ   Now, if you're gonna quote my record, sir, you gotta quote the whole thing. I'm a Roosevelt New Dealer at heart. As a matter of fact, John F. Kennedy was a little *too* conservative for my taste.

MLK   I don't need to tell you how significant the Negro vote was in President Kennedy's election.

LBJ   President Kennedy was always very appreciative of your vote.

MLK   He didn't have my vote. (*off LBJ's look*) Georgia officials declared I hadn't lived long enough in Atlanta and Alabama officials said it was too late to vote absentee. Voting Rights matter, Mr. President. Nothing will ever really change in this country until Negroes can vote.

LBJ   The next Bill will be Voting Rights.

MLK   After President Kennedy's election, Eisenhower publicly declared that his party had taken the Negro vote for granted. I would hate to see the Democratic Party make the same mistake.

LBJ   If you think Barry Goldwater is a legitimate heir to Abraham Lincoln, then you should vote for him! Civil rights is not the only thing I'm interested in, Dr. King. We got people in this country livin' in unbelievable poverty. I know, I grew up like that in the Hill Country. Picking cotton on my hands and knees. Harnessed like a mule to a road plow. Living off the bitter charity of my neighbors. No silver spoon in my mouth like Bobby Kennedy! But I gotta dream, see, where we change all that. We are gonna declare a "War on Poverty" and by God, we're gonna beat it!

MLK   A War on Poverty?

LBJ   That's right! I got all kinds of Federal programs in mind on Health, Education, Literacy, Jobs, you name it. We're gonna change this country, top to bottom!

MLK   That sounds—extraordinary.

LBJ   There you go!

MLK   I would *very* enthusiastically support legislation to that effect but—right now—I need to be able to go back to my people and tell them that this President is committed to *civil rights* and that this Bill, even without voting rights, will still be a strong Bill, with *no further changes*. If I can't do that, I will lose their faith, and in their despair, I don't know what will happen.

LBJ   Is that a threat?

MLK   Certainly not. I don't want any spontaneous demonstrations in the street any more than you do but in order to avoid that kind of situation I need to be able to deliver meaningful reform.

LBJ   OK. OK, here's what I need. The Bill is stuck in Judge Smith's Rules Committee . . . Walter! . . . (*back to King*) . . . and I need at least eight votes to pry it out. 5 Republicans and 3 Democrats. WALTER!

Walter runs in.

Gimme that list of names. (*Walter hands him the list.*) You get your people in each of these districts, your ministers, clergy, Union supporters, and what have you, to lobby these Representatives to release that Bill. (*hands list to MLK*) Lobbyin' is just like propositioning women, you know?

MLK hesitates. Is this a coded reference to his own philandering?

MLK   I'm not sure I understand.

LBJ I knew this fella once, a real ladies man, got more pussy than you ever saw, and I said to him, "What's your secret?" And he said he'd go into a bar and ask each woman if she wanted to go out. "Boy, you musta got slapped a lot," I said. "Oh, hell, yeah," he says, "but I also got me a lot of yeses." We only need eight yeses to get it out of Judge Smith's committee.

A moment.

MLK Alright.

LBJ Alright.

LIGHTS shift. UP on **REPRESENTATIVE "JUDGE" SMITH**.

REP. JUDGE SMITH You invite me over here, Mr. President, to apply the ole Texas Twist?

A **BLACK BUTLER** *serves both men drinks.*

LBJ Don't believe everything you hear, Judge; we're just two old friends talking over a glass of Cutty. Now, you've done a helluva job bottling up that Bill in Committee, and I reckon all the folks back home will know you for a man who stands up for his beliefs, but it's time to turn it loose now.

REP. JUDGE SMITH In good conscience, I don't think I can do that, Mr. President.

LBJ This is a popular Bill, Judge. It's bad for the Democratic party to be seen blocking it.

REP. JUDGE SMITH Then you should get a Discharge Petition but if you had those votes in the House, I guess we wouldn't be having this conversation.

LBJ Well, you're right about that. Which is why I've decided to move the Bill out on a *procedural vote*. I have 11 votes *from your Committee* to send the Bill to the floor.

A moment.

REP. JUDGE SMITH   Bullshit.

LBJ hands him a piece of paper.

LBJ   You know what was surprisin'? It wasn't all that hard to line up the votes against you. Now, how is that gonna play back home, Judge, your own Committee over-ridin' its Chairman? Some people will no doubt be suggestin' that maybe you're gettin' too old for all this. The DNC was just on me the other day sayin' maybe we oughta start lookin' at some young blood in Virginia but I told them, NO, I said, Judge Smith is a team player and he's gonna do the right thing! Isn't he? Freshen that drink for you?

TB reads: **CIVIL RIGHTS BILL MOVES TO HOUSE!**

LIGHTS UP on hotel room and meeting of the Council for Federated Organizations (COFO). Present are MLK, RALPH ABERNATHY, BOB MOSES (SNCC), STOKELY CARMICHAEL (SNCC), and ROY WILKINS (NAACP).

In a SPOT US, we see **FBI AGENTS** *secretly tape-recording scene.*

MLK   He said he'd get it out of Committee and by God, he did.

STOKELY CARMICHAEL   And all it cost us was the Voting Rights section. Hell, let's just declare victory and go home!

ROY WILKINS   If you spent a little less time in the backwoods of Mississippi, Stokely, and a little more time in the back halls of Congress, maybe you would understand how things work.

STOKELY CARMICHAEL   Oh, I understand how things work, Mista Wilkins. The House nigra always thinks he's better then the field nigra.

ROY WILKINS   Don't you get up on your hind legs with me. I was working for the Cause while your mother was still wiping your ass.

STOKELY CARMICHAEL   And accomplishing what, exactly? I mean aside from getting yourself invited to the White House for tea.

ROY WILKINS	STOKELY CARMICHAEL
Every major legislative and judicial victory of the last fifty years has been the work of the NAACP!	It wasn't until Negroes took to the streets, that we started to get things done in this country. SNCC did that! *SNCC did that!*

ROY WILKINS Like the deaths of those four little girls in Birmingham.

STOKELY CARMICHAEL Oh, I see, we gonna blame the victim for the lynching!

MLK Gentlemen, this is not helpful! Given our success extracting the Bill from Judge Smith's committee, the President has asked for our continued assistance in lobbying Congress.

BOB MOSES Do we have to endorse his candidacy as well?

MLK (*smiling*) Are you leaning Republican this election, Bob? Goldwater came out against civil rights.

RALPH ABERNATHY (*sarcastic*) Purely on Constitutional grounds, you understand—personally Goldwater deplores racism.

STOKELY CARMICHAEL I think asking for my vote while denying me the right to vote is bullshit.

ROY WILKINS The Bill still gives us a lot.

BOB MOSES Unless he gives that away, too.

MLK I have his word there will be no more compromises.

STOKELY CARMICHAEL "His word?" Are you serious?

MLK He's made Humphrey floor manager of the bill.

RALPH ABERNATHY And you know he's on our side.

MLK And Johnson knows that if he breaks his promise, there will be demonstrations all over the country.

ROY WILKINS No, there will most certainly not be!

MLK   Until this Bill passes, Roy, we have to hold his feet to the fire! While he's running for election he doesn't want us in the street.

RALPH ABERNATHY   And that's the leverage we have.

BOB MOSES (*to MLK*)   · It's only a threat if you're willing to use it, Doc. If he doesn't deliver, will you support a public action?

MLK   I will be in the street myself. Now, will SNCC work with us?

BOB MOSES   I can't support a Bill without Voting Rights.

MLK   I'm not asking you to. I'm asking you *not to work against it.* Look, the President is also planning new legislation that will bring a huge Federal intervention in Poverty, Hunger, and *Jobs.* Think about what that would mean to our people.

ROY WILKINS   He said that to you?

MLK   He called it a "War on Poverty."

STOKELY CARMICHAEL   Forty acres and a mule. What if he's just sweet talkin' you until the election?

MLK   What if he's serious?

STOKELY looks to MOSES.

BOB MOSES   OK. We won't campaign against the Bill. *For now.* But SNCC isn't gonna ring any doorbells for LBJ neither.

MLK   Fair enough.

BOB MOSES   But we're not gonna sit on our hands.

ROY WILKINS   And what does the visionary Bob Moses propose?

BOB MOSES   "Freedom Summer." We are going to send hundreds of student volunteers down to Mississippi, flood the state with our people, to educate and register Negro voters.

RALPH ABERNATHY (*stunned*)   Mississippi?

ROY WILKINS   You are out of your ever-loving mind.

41

STOKELY CARMICHAEL Not just black volunteers. White students, too.

ROY WILKINS Worse and worse. If just one of your white volunteers gets hurt, you will do irreparable damage to the Cause.

STOKELY CARMICHAEL Whereas if one of our Negro volunteers gets hurt, who gives a fuck? Yeah, there may be trouble. *That's the point*, isn't it? When Dr. King talks about "surfacing evil for all the world to see" what he means is deliberately provoking some red-neck to bust my head on National TV.

RALPH ABERNATHY That's an absurd reduction of Dr. King's philosophy!

STOKELY CARMICHAEL The Birmingham campaign was dying until you put children on the street in harm's way. Dogs biting kids. Children being blasted with fire hoses. That got the press all excited, didn't it? That got the President's attention. If it takes some white kid getting smacked around to shed just a little light on the darkness that is Mississippi, well why not?

ROY WILKINS Because people will die in Mississippi.

STOKELY CARMICHAEL People are dying in Mississippi!

ROY WILKINS Those deaths will be on your head! I cannot support this!

BOB MOSES Nobody's asking for your permission, Roy!

MLK Alright, alright! Let's calm down. I think we can all agree that nobody here is gonna have to do something they can't get behind, but there's nothing that says we can't move ahead on multiple fronts at the same time. We should respond to the elimination of voting rights, and Freedom Summer is a great way to do that. At the same time, Roy, you're right, the Bill still gives us a lot. Nobody in this room has your legislative experience. Clearly, you and the NAACP should take the lead on our lobbying effort in DC.

RALPH ABERNATHY   Meanwhile, SCLC will mobilize religious leaders and our labor allies to bring pressure to bear at home.

MLK   That way we're not gonna give them a moment's rest.

RALPH ABERNATHY   Anywhere.

BOB MOSES   We need funding.

Wilkins laughs.

ROY WILKINS   Here it comes. Big talk, then both hands out!

MLK   We'll help.

RALPH ABERNATHY   . . . Martin, how are we gonna . . .

MLK (*sharply*)   . . . just arrange a few more speeches, Ralph.

RALPH ABERNATHY   When? You're already . . .

MLK   At this point what difference does it make?! (*to Moses*) All right?

A moment. Moses nods. King looks to Wilkins.

All right?

Wilkins nods reluctantly. A moment.

RALPH ABERNATHY   Gentlemen?

Moses, Wilkins and Stokely leave.

One of these days, Stokely and Wilkins are just gonna kill each other, right there in the middle of the room.

MLK   Well, in that case, we'll sell tickets and maybe I can stop giving speeches.

They both laugh; their momentary estrangement forgotten.

RALPH ABERNATHY   Your meeting tomorrow morning with the Catholic Interracial Council has been moved to 8:00 AM. Car will take you to the airport afterwards for your speech in Cincinnati to the International Union of Laundry Workers. Afternoon flight to Cleveland and the United Synagogue of America dinner. Next morning is Western Michigan University. You need anything?

MLK   I'm fine.

RALPH ABERNATHY   Good night then.

Abernathy leaves. MLK pours a drink. The bedroom door opens. In the spill of light, a beautiful **WOMAN** *stands there, smiling suggestively at MLK.*

WOMAN   Is the coast clear?

MLK smiles at her.

MLK   Give me a minute?

WOMAN   When you're ready.

She goes back into the room.

MLK drinks. LIGHTS DOWN on room. SPOT lingers on FBI agent—SPOT UP on Hoover/Deloach. Hoover holds aloft a reel of incriminating tape.

J. EDGAR HOOVER (*triumphant*)   THIS TAPE WILL KILL THE BURR-HEAD! I want a "highlights" reel sent over to Walter Jenkins at the White House immediately. There's no way the President can ignore this!

LIGHTS shift to Oval Office. LBJ walks in with headphones on, listening to the sex tapes with delight.

LBJ   The sex-mad preacher.

J. EDGAR HOOVER   His hypocrisy is disgusting!

Laughing, LBJ takes off his headphones.

His hypocrisy is disgusting. The man is a flagrant adulterer.

LBJ   Oh my, a Southern preacher who screws his choir. Who ever heard of that? Jay, if you arrested every politician and preacher who

44

strayed from the marital bed wouldn't be nobody in Congress or the pulpit. Whatever a man gets up to in his privacy is his own business.

J. EDGAR HOOVER   His moral turpitude is just the tip of the iceberg! I am sure . . .

LBJ (*cutting him off*)   Jay. Far be it from me to tell you how to do your job, so, keep an eye on him, sure, but while I'm trying to get this Bill passed, *this is not helpful*, you understand me?

J. EDGAR HOOVER   Yes, sir.

LBJ leaves. Deloach approaches quietly.

DEKE DELOACH   Call off the surveillance teams?

A moment.

J. EDGAR HOOVER   It's our job to protect the President from his enemies. And from himself. *Expand our surveillance*; find me another way to expose King. (*stops and considers*) Maybe a word with one of our good friends in the Press.

SPOT DOWN on Hoover/Deloach.

TB reads: **HOUSE OF REPRESENTATIVES. 8 MONTHS TO THE ELECTION.**

Witnesses assemble facing audience. SPOTS pick out individuals as they "address" the House, speaking directly to the audience. LBJ watches carefully from the upper gallery.

SPEAKER JOHN MCCORMACK (D-MA)   We will now call the House of Representatives to order to consider House Bill 736, the Civil Rights Act of 1964.

REP. JUDGE SMITH (D-VA)   This Bill is nothing less than an assault on the Constitution by the Federal Government. Who are we to tell the owner of a cafe who he can hire and who he can serve? Who are we to tell a state that they may not pass segregation laws?

REP. EMANUEL CELLER (D-NY)   Congress not only has the legal right to pass such a law, it has the moral responsibility to ensure equality for *all*.

REP. WILLIAM COLMER (D-MISS)   Congress is allowin' itself to be stampeded on this issue out of fear! Are we to yield to threats of demonstrations, even riots, by minority groups—"blackmail," if you will?

REP. BILL MCCULLOCH (R-OHIO)   Not fear, but belief in the equality of man induces me to support this legislation. As a conservative Republican, I believe that state authority should not be needlessly usurped by a centralized government but I also believe that the Constitution doesn't say that whites alone shall have our basic rights, but that we *all* shall have them.

REP. JUDGE SMITH (D-VA)   I would like to introduce an amendment here that would exempt local businesses in public accommodations. For instance, if you were a Chiropodist and had your office in a hotel. If I were cuttin' corns I would want to know whose feet I would have to be monkeyin' around with. I would want to know whether they smelled good or bad. Chiropodists, like other minorities, got rights, too. To force them to work violates the Thirteenth Amendment's prohibition against slavery or involuntary servitude!

REP. JAMES CORMAN (D-CA)   I, for one, am fed up with amendments that subtly or blatantly defeat the purpose of this Bill.

REP. KATHARINE ST. GEORGE   Thank you!

REP. JAMES CORMAN (D-CA)   To my esteemed colleague, Representative Smith, if you are going to trim the stinky, sweaty white corns, you must do the same with the black ones!

*All turn to look at the Tally Board which changes to read: **149 AGAINST—107 FOR**.*

SPEAKER JOHN MCCORMACK   The Amendment is defeated!

Smith refuses to give up.

REP. JUDGE SMITH   Very well. I would like to introduce a new amendment forbiddin' discrimination based on *Sex*.

REP. EMANUEL CELLER (*shouting*)   Gender has nothing to do with discrimination! There are basic differences between Men and Women.

REP. JUDGE SMITH   Yes, I'm happily aware of the differences. I simply feel that while we're doin' "Good" here, that White, Christian, Anglo-Saxon women not be the only group left unprotected.

REP. EMANUEL CELLER   In my memory, Sex has never been an issue in the civil rights bill!

REP. KATHARINE ST. GEORGE (R-NY)   It is possible, given the age of the Chairman, that sex itself may be no more than a distant memory. (*Everyone laughs*) I, for one, support this amendment forbidding discrimination based on Gender and I encourage my colleagues to do so!

*All turn to look at the Tally Board which changes to read: **168 FOR— 133 AGAINST**.*

SPEAKER JOHN MCCORMACK   The Amendment passes! With no more amendments to be offered, the Speaker calls for a final vote on House Bill 736.

*Everyone turns to look at the Tally Board. **290 FOR—130 AGAINST**.*

SPEAKER MCCORMACK   THE BILL PASSES AND WILL NOW GO TO THE SENATE!

Applause. Stage empties except for the Southern caucus members who angrily surround Senator Russell as he gets his shoes shined.

SENATOR JIM EASTLAND   "Trust LBJ! He's one of us!"

SENATOR RUSSELL   He cut Voting Rights, didn't he?

SENATOR STROM THURMOND   But he didn't kill the Bill.

SENATOR RUSSELL   One step at a time.

REP. JUDGE SMITH   He threatened me with my goddamn Committee Chairmanship! Did you know he was gonna do that?

SENATOR RUSSELL (*surprised*)   Lyndon can—over-react at times. That's no excuse, mind you, but let's be honest, is this the first time a civil rights bill has made it through the House? Don't worry, the President will be there when we need him.

SENATOR STROM THURMOND   All I know is, the Republican nominee's views on this Bill are a whole lot closer to my position than the Democratic nominee.

REP. JUDGE SMITH   *Presumptive* Democratic nominee.

SENATOR RUSSELL   Now that's just foolishness talkin'.

SENATOR JIM EASTLAND   Wallace took a third of the vote in both Wisconsin and Indiana, and he's runnin' strong in Maryland.

SENATOR RUSSELL   That's like a tick on the hind end of a mule thinkin' he's in charge. Lyndon Johnson is gonna be the Democratic candidate come Atlantic City! And don't talk to me, Strom, about Barry Goldwater. That man is no friend of the South.

SENATOR STROM THURMOND   The enemy of my enemy is my friend.

SENATOR RUSSELL   The Republican Party is never gonna be a friend to the South! Goldwater's opposed to Social Security and Farm Supports. You think your people are gonna like that? Alright, so the Bill goes to the Senate. So what? As long as we stick together, we'll be fine. First they gotta get the Bill outta Jim's Committee. (*to Eastland*) How many civil rights bills you buried in the last ten years?

SENATOR JIM EASTLAND   One hundred and twenty-one.

SENATOR RUSSELL   Has that "graveyard" of yours got room for one more?

SENATOR JIM EASTLAND   I'm diggin' a hole as we speak.

SENATOR RUSSELL   Alright then.

Russell rises and pays the **SHOE SHINE MAN** *throughout the following.*

SENATOR STROM THURMOND   But what if Lyndon gets it outta Committee and onto the Senate floor? What then?

SENATOR RUSSELL   Then we'll *filibuster* it, Strom, like we've done a thousand times before. It won't take much. Not with a National Election coming up and everybody needing to get back home to his campaign. And I think public opinion is already turning against this Bill, particularly in the North with these riots!

LIGHTS DOWN on Southern caucus. LIGHTS UP on Wallace and Lurleen in Maryland being pursued by **REPORTERS**. *A Camera projects his image on the TB. Sounds of a riot in the background.*

REPORTERS   Governor!/Governor Wallace!/Over here, Governor!

REPORTER #1   Governor, some people blame your appearance here in Maryland for these race riots. How do you respond to those charges?

GOVERNOR GEORGE WALLACE   I don't accept them at all. Lurleen and I are just sick about what's happened here 'cause we don't have any of this kinda business in Alabama. If somebody were to try and start a riot down there, the first one to pick up a brick would get a bullet in the brain. You shoot a few of these fellas and you got that mess stopped cold. Now President Johnson prob'ly wouldn't advocate that. 'Course I don't see him around here, do you? He's the one stirred up this pot with this so-called "civil rights" bill but left the rest of us to clean up his mess.

REPORTER #2   How would you do that, Governor? "Clean up his mess?"

GOVERNOR GEORGE WALLACE   Just plain common sense. Listen to the People. The American people are fed up with this continuin' trend toward a socialist state which subjects the individual to the dictates of an all-powerful central government! I am runnin' for

49

President because I was born free. I want to remain free. And I want your children and mine to stay free!

LIGHTS fade down on Wallace and up on LBJ/Humphrey/Walter in Oval Office watching Wallace on TV.

SENATOR HUBERT HUMPHREY Wallace's support with Whites in the Eastern part of Maryland is running ninety percent. If he wins that primary, Senators who've been in favor of the Bill are going to vote against it.

LBJ Wallace would be dead in the water without these damn riots. Christ's sake, King was supposed to control his people!

SENATOR HUBERT HUMPHREY I don't think he can. I did warn you that cutting Voting Rights was going to be unpopular.

LBJ Don't you dare lecture me.

SENATOR HUBERT HUMPHREY I'm just saying . . .

LBJ . . . we wouldn't even have a goddamn Bill if I hadn't cut it! Put my entire political career at risk for the nigras and this is the thanks I get?

SENATOR HUBERT HUMPHREY There's a whole new generation of young people out there who don't listen to anybody, including Dr. King.

*A **BARBER** enters and begins trimming LBJ's hair throughout the following.*

LBJ Well, somebody sure as hell needs to crack some heads and get those folks in line.

WALTER JENKINS Put more money into the Maryland primary?

LBJ *(nodding)* And beef up my schedule there. *(to Humphrey)* What's your plan to get our Bill out of Jim Eastland's Judiciary Committee?

SENATOR HUBERT HUMPHREY Discharge Petition.

LBJ You don't have the votes.

SENATOR HUBERT HUMPHREY   I think we might be close.

LBJ   "Close" don't mean shit. You don't have the goddamn votes.

SENATOR HUBERT HUMPHREY   I don't know then; what's your idea?

LBJ   I don't know but I'll think of something. OK, let's say we find a way to clear the Committee. What does Russell do then?

SENATOR HUBERT HUMPHREY (*on safer ground*)   He'll filibuster the Bill.

LBJ   How do you defeat the filibuster?

SENATOR HUBERT HUMPHREY   We need to cross the aisle and pick up at least twenty-five Republican votes in order to get a two-thirds majority and force Cloture.

LBJ   How?

SENATOR HUBERT HUMPHREY   Go right at the Republicans. You're either for civil rights or you're not. You're either the party of Lincoln or you're not. And if you're not, get over there with racists like Jim Eastland and Judge Smith.

LBJ (*laughing*)   Jesus Christ, no, Hubert. They got to join us *willingly*. We got to make this an *American* bill; not just a Democrat bill. And you don't need twenty-five Republican votes. You need ONE Republican vote.

SENATOR HUBERT HUMPHREY   Senator Dirksen.

LBJ   Right. You get the Senate Minority Leader on board and the troops will follow. How?

SENATOR HUBERT HUMPHREY (*hesitantly*)   Dirksen has already announced his opposition to the two most important provisions: Public Accommodation and Employment Discrimination. Surely, we have to challenge him.

LBJ   Now, that's just foolishness. You don't want to get his back up. Let me tell you about Senator Everett Dirksen. That man is in love with himself; in love with his *voice*. Did you know that every day he gargles with warm water and Pond's beauty cream? I shit you not. Now, a man like that wants one thing—he wants to be a "Great Man." And you're gonna give him every opportunity to do just that. Every chance you get, you praise Dirksen, you thank Dirksen. You're gonna kiss his ass so much, he won't be able to sit down. He wants the spotlight? *Give it to him.* Six months from now, all anybody will remember is that the Democratic Party passed a historic civil rights bill.

SENATOR HUBERT HUMPHREY   So . . . how *do* we get the Bill out of the Senate Judiciary Committee?

LBJ   I can't roll Jim Eastland like I done Judge Smith, I'll tell you that. Dick Russell is gonna have all his dogs on a short leash now.

SENATOR HUBERT HUMPHREY   There's nobody stronger on Constitutional law than Russell.

LBJ   That's got nothin' to do with it. This battle's gonna be fought where it's always been fought, on *the Rules of the Senate* and Dick Russell's been studyin' them since he was suckin' on his momma's titty. I've seen him make a fool of you Liberals with some arcane Rule of Order more times than I can remember. There was that . . .

LBJ suddenly rises with excitement; whips the barber's towel off his neck.

Hold on. Hold on now. Shit. There *is* a way we can completely bypass Eastland's Committee without either a Discharge Petition OR a Procedural Vote. Nobody's ever done it this way but it just might work.

SENATOR HUBERT HUMPHREY   How do you do that?

LBJ   With the rules of the Senate. You appear to be giving in and waive a second reading of the Bill on the floor.

SENATOR HUBERT HUMPHREY (*confused*) That automatically sends the Bill back to Committee.

LBJ Ordinarily it would but what if, instead, you suddenly have the Senate Majority Leader reverse course and call for a straight up or down vote to put the Bill on the Senate calendar? Russell won't be expecting that.

SENATOR HUBERT HUMPHREY (*putting it together*) Because there's no precedent.

LBJ *No precedent.* And in the absence of any established precedent, a Bill *automatically* bypasses Committee and . . .

SENATOR HUBERT HUMPHREY . . . *goes straight to the Senate!* That's brilliant.

LBJ shrugs; moody again.

SENATOR HUBERT HUMPHREY You don't seem very happy about it.

LBJ These things always come with a cost.

LIGHTS SHIFT. The White House. Russell, LBJ, and Lady Bird share an informal dinner. The men are polite but very tense.

LADY BIRD JOHNSON Would you like some more gravy, Uncle Dick?

SENATOR RUSSELL It was delicious, Lady Bird, but no, I couldn't possibly.

LBJ What about me, aren't you going to offer me any more gravy?

LADY BIRD JOHNSON (*cautiously*) Well, honey, I'd like to but I can't.

LBJ (*to Russell*) Bird has me on a *diet.* Got Zephyr in there in the kitchen weighing my plate 'fore every meal. Ridiculous! Pork chops are just an excuse for gravy. Without gravy, I don't see the point, do you? Might as well eat cardboard.

SENATOR RUSSELL Your wife just doesn't want to see you get too big for your britches, an entirely understandable concern.

Silence. Lady Bird rises nervously.

LADY BIRD JOHNSON I think I'll go see how Zephyr's coming with that cobbler.

As soon as Lady Bird is gone, both men drop any pretense of politeness.

SENATOR RUSSELL Pretty slick what you did with Jim's committee, getting that Bill out.

LBJ Everything I know, you taught me, Dick.

SENATOR RUSSELL I also taught you somethin' about Party loyalty.

LBJ The Party is changin' and we got to change with it. This younger generation's not gonna fall on their swords for segregation; they want to get re-elected. If you think they'll stick with you to the end, you'll be disappointed.

SENATOR RUSSELL If you think all Southerners are suddenly gonna start dancin' to your tune, you're the one who's gonna be disappointed. Wallace almost won Maryland.

LBJ But he didn't.

SENATOR RUSSELL But he *almost* did. Times *are* changin' but maybe not the way you think.

LBJ It doesn't have to be this way, Dick.

SENATOR RUSSELL You're thinking you can cut a deal with Dirksen, aren't you?

LBJ You filibuster the Senate, what choice do you leave me? Allow the Bill to come to a vote.

SENATOR RUSSELL A Democratic President ignorin' his own party and makin' a deal with Senate Republicans.

LBJ Now, don't get all high and mighty with me! You and those conservative Republicans been cuttin' deals for years. That's how you've de-nutted every civil rights bill that's come down the pike, but now I can't cross the aisle? We don't have to fight, Dick.

SENATOR RUSSELL   Some people will eventually yield to overwhelmin' force and quit fightin'. I won't.

LBJ (*softly*)   I'm coming for you, Dick. I love you more'n my own daddy but if you get in my way, I'll crush you.

LIGHTS SHIFT as Russell moves into a SPOT addressing Reporters. LBJ watches.

SENATOR RUSSELL   I regret that the President has embraced the radical program of the left-wing groups that is erroneously called the "civil rights bill." It is still a vicious assault on the Constitution and we in the Senate intend to fight this bill with our boots on to the last ditch. Beginning today, we will filibuster this Bill! *Let the real war begin!*

Russell exits. SPOT brightens on LBJ.

LBJ (*to the Audience*)   "Defending the Constitution." Let me tell you what we're really talkin' 'bout here. My first year outta college the only job I could get was teachin' first grade in a beat up old elementary school in Cotulla, Texas, a dusty border town in the middle of nowhere, full of wetback Mexicans who didn't have a pot to piss in. But God, did I love those kids of mine. They would show up every mornin', dirty, ragged, and hungry 'cause most of 'em hadn't had breakfast but they were so on fire to learn it just made you feel good. But for each one of them, there would come a day when I would see the light in their eyes die because they had discovered that the world hated 'em just because of the color of their skin. All my life as a Southerner I've had to bite my tongue on this issue 'till my mouth was fulla blood. Not anymore. What's the point of bein' President if you can't do what you know is right? This ain't about the Constitution. This is about those who got more, wantin' to hang on to what they got, at the expense of those who got *nothin'*. And feel good about it. Uncle Dick can talk about his Rights 'till he's blue in the face but all I see are the faces of those little kids in Cotulla. He's right about one thing though; the war has just begun.

LIGHTS UP on MLK/Abernathy in hotel. Jenkins joins LBJ in Oval Office and hands him a newspaper.

MLK   The press accuses me of lying to Congress about my "associations" AND having an unnamed advisor who is . . .

MLK/LBJ *(reading from paper)*   "Known to be a senior figure in the covert apparatus of the Communist Party!"

MLK   They're goin' after Stanley.

LBJ *(furious)*   This has got Hoover's fingerprints all over it.

RALPH ABERNATHY   It's garbage, Martin.

WALTER JENKINS   It's garbage, Mr. President.

MLK   It's not garbage when it's printed in the *Washington Post!*

LBJ   It may be garbage but it could derail the whole damn Bill. The Southern caucus is gonna be all over this like stink on shit. "Civil rights and Communists!" Hell, if the Mississippi river flooded tomorrow, Jim Eastland would declare it was the work of niggers and Reds.

RALPH ABERNATHY   Ignore it.

WALTER JENKINS   Maybe you should just ignore it.

MLK   This is Hoover!

LBJ   This is Hoover!

LBJ   I wish to God I understood why Jay has such a stick up his ass for that man!

MLK   Why is he persecuting me?

RALPH ABERNATHY   Don't respond. Don't bring it any more attention than it deserves.

LIGHTS down on Abernathy/MLK.

LBJ   This is just what Russell needs to fuel his filibuster and it'll make Dirksen that much more skittish about breaking ranks. Tell Jay I need to see him right away.

LIGHTS shift. Hoover enters.

J. EDGAR HOOVER   Mr. President?

LBJ makes him wait then . . .

LBJ   What do you think of this civil rights bill of mine?

J. EDGAR HOOVER *(cautiously)*   I think—it's historic.

LBJ   You favor integration?

J. EDGAR HOOVER   I am proud to say I integrated the FBI several years ago.

LBJ   You did?

J. EDGAR HOOVER   Yes sir, we have two Negro agents. They drive my car.

LBJ   Uh-huh. Well, I'm glad to hear of your enthusiasm for this Bill because it's important to me, you understand. Important. *To me.* And anythin' that gets in the way is not helpful. Like this column in the paper. Where do you suppose that came from?

J. EDGAR HOOVER   I have no idea, Mr. President, but there are many people who feel that King is not a man to be trusted.

LBJ   Yes, we talked about the tapes.

J. EDGAR HOOVER   His adultery is just the tip of the iceberg. I have voluminous proof of his numerous contacts over the years with active Communist agents.

LBJ   This "Levison" fella, right? Says who?

J. EDGAR HOOVER   I'm sorry?

LBJ   Who says he's an active Communist agent? You make these accusations but I never see the actual reports. Why is that?

J. EDGAR HOOVER (*hesitating*)   Mr. President, these are very—very delicate issues. These sources—are a matter of National Security and could be easily compromised, undoing decades of work.

LBJ   Are you sayin' you can't tell me, the President of the United States, the source of these allegations? (*Hoover is silent.*) How old are you, Jay?

J. EDGAR HOOVER (*surprised*)   How old?

LBJ   Seventy somethin', isn't it?

J. EDGAR HOOVER   I'm sixty-nine.

LBJ   Sixty-nine. Uh-huh. You know, people are sayin' you're gonna retire next year.

J. EDGAR HOOVER (*panicked*)   That's not true. Not true at all.

LBJ   God knows you've carried a heavy burden all these years.

J. EDGAR HOOVER   I'm in excellent health.

LBJ   Of course you'll be retiring on a full salary.

J. EDGAR HOOVER   I've never forgotten your help in that matter.

LBJ   Loyal service should be rewarded. We'll miss you, of course.

J. EDGAR HOOVER   But I feel I can still be of service to my country; service to you, Mr. President. Just as I dealt with that perjured witness in the Billie Sol Estes scandal when your name came up . . .

LBJ (*alarms going off*)   . . . Now, that's goin' back a ways . . .

J. EDGAR HOOVER   . . . there are any number of unscrupulous people out there who don't wish you well, the Robert Kennedys of the world, and others, many others, who are ready to pass on the most outrageous, damaging kinds of gossip about your financial dealings; rumors of sexual relationships. I keep careful track of these things to protect you, Mr. President, and without me, who can say what might happen?

A moment

If that's all, sir?

LBJ nods; Hoover leaves.

LBJ (*quietly*)   Son of a bitch.

WALTER JENKINS   The problem, as I see it, Mr. President, is this Levison character. If he goes away, what leverage does the Director have?

A moment.

LBJ   You know, Walter, every once in a while you have your moments.

LIGHTS down on LBJ/Jenkins, UP on MLK/Abernathy.

MLK   He is my friend!

RALPH ABERNATHY   And a member of the Communist party.

MLK   A *former member* who left in disgust many years ago.

RALPH ABERNATHY   A distinction not always appreciated by the public.

MLK   Don't we preach forgiveness?

RALPH ABERNATHY   This isn't about Salvation, Martin, it's about politics.

MLK   I value his advice. And his service. He's given everything he has . . .

RALPH ABERNATHY   . . . I didn't say it was fair.

MLK   *He is my friend.*

RALPH ABERNATHY   *He is a liability.* The President has made that very clear. He is a way to attack you and what you believe. Is it worth that?

MLK   Not everything can be weighed by that scale.

RALPH ABERNATHY   The Bill, Martin. *The Bill.* We are a "Sacrificial Movement"; *your words.* What is really important here?

A moment.

MLK   You remember that Klan bombing in Montgomery that just barely missed killing Coretta and my baby? I never told you this. Never told anybody. But after the police had come and gone, I sat up alone in what was left of my kitchen, over a cold cup of coffee. It was midnight by then and the phone rang. Some other hate-filled voice telling me, "Nigger, we are tired of you and your mess now. If you aren't gone in three days, we're gonna blow your brains out." And I realized there was nobody I could turn to for help. Not really. Nobody. And I bowed my head down and I prayed out loud, saying, Lord, I'm down here trying to do what is right but I'm weak now. I am losing my courage. And then, I heard an inner voice saying to me, stand up for Truth and lo, I will be with you even until the end of the world. He promised never to leave me; never to leave me alone. Will He still be with us, if we abandon others?

Abernathy leaves. Levison enters. LIGHTS UP simultaneously on LBJ and Hoover in Rose Garden in front of Reporters.

STANLEY LEVISON   This was always a possibility, Martin.

MLK   It's red-baiting! Whenever they feel like we're getting too uppity, they drag out the ghost of some fucking Communist conspiracy.

LBJ   I just want to take this opportunity to reflect on Director J. Edgar Hoover's extraordinary and unblemished record of service to this country. Forty years.

STANLEY LEVISON   It's just politics.

LBJ   And Mr. Hoover, I know I speak for all Americans when I say, I hope you're with us for another forty!

Hoover smiles.

STANLEY LEVISON   They don't win, Martin, unless we quit.

LIGHTS OUT on Hoover/LBJ. Levison leaves. LIGHTS up on Humphrey. MLK joins him. TB reads: **7 MONTHS TO THE ELECTION.**

MLK   *Is the President caving in?* I would ask him myself but he's no longer returning my phone calls.

SENATOR HUBERT HUMPHREY   Absolutely not.

MLK   I have made every painful sacrifice that's been asked of me: releasing Stanley Levison; convincing the other Movement leaders to support the President-even after he cut Voting Rights; putting all our precious resources into lobbying on his behalf; and the Bill is still stuck in the Senate.

SENATOR HUBERT HUMPHREY   I'm as frustrated as you are, Martin, but lining up the votes to break the filibuster is a complicated process . . .

MLK   . . . And now these *new amendments* of Dirksen's!

SENATOR HUBERT HUMPHREY   I know, I know.

MLK   If you accept these changes, there won't be demonstrations, there will be a Negro revolution.

SENATOR HUBERT HUMPHREY   We're all on the same side here.

MLK   Are we? If this is what it takes to move this Bill, I will start a *public fast to the death.*

SENATOR HUBERT HUMPHREY (*worried*)   Martin, please, God, that's not necessary.

MLK   No? I have put all my credibility on the line telling our young people that yes, this President can be trusted, but they don't see any difference between Dirksen's Amendments and Bull Connor's billy clubs. They want *results.* They are in Mississippi right now putting their lives at risk registering Negroes for a vote they still don't have!

SENATOR HUBERT HUMPHREY   We've already talked Dirksen down from his original seventy amendments to forty.

MLK   The amendments he gave up were meaningless; we gave up Voting Rights!

SENATOR HUBERT HUMPHREY   Dirksen has to make it look like he's fighting the good fight.

MLK   His remaining amendments will gut the bill. *I would rather have no bill at all than what he proposes!*

SENATOR HUBERT HUMPHREY   Look, I want a good bill, too, but you can't give people blood tests for Loyalty every fifteen minutes! The President will handle Everett Dirksen, I promise you.

LIGHTS DOWN on Humphrey/MLK. LIGHTS UP on Oval Office. A very confident, **SENATOR DIRKSEN** *enters.*

SENATOR DIRKSEN   Mr. President.

LBJ   Everett, what's this bullshit about how I treat my dog?!

SENATOR DIRKSEN (*confused*)   I'm sorry?

LBJ   My dog! Little Beagle Johnson. Why are you being such a shit-heel with the press about me pulling his ears? The little sumbitch loves to have his ears pulled! Hell, I thought you were running the Senate Republicans, not the ASPCA!

SENATOR DIRKSEN   Mr. President, I was just kidding with the Press about that.

LBJ   Well, don't! I'm a helluva lot better than you are with dogs, dogs and people. You know the best thing about the White House? Your damn dog can't run off . . .

SENATOR DIRKSEN   . . . Yes, sir. I was hoping we could talk . . .

LBJ   . . . You called me about appointin' William McComber as Ambassador.

SENATOR DIRKSEN   Among other things. I was hoping we . . .

LBJ   . . . We'll get to that other stuff in a minute. *McComber.*

SENATOR DIRKSEN   He's a very good man.

LBJ   I don't care if he's a good man. There are a million Johnson men who are good guys but if I'm appointin' a Republican ambassador, it better be Senator Everett Dirksen's Republican Ambassador. So, do you want this guy appointed?

SENATOR DIRKSEN   Yes, I do.

LBJ   Done. Everett, we got to get this civil rights bill passed. The longer this filibuster goes, the stronger Russell and his people get, and the angrier those Negroes on the street are. We know how many votes we got for cloture on our side—how many will we get from your people?

SENATOR DIRKSEN   Well, that's, that's what I wanted to talk to you about, Mr. President. I have a hell of a problem with my side.

LBJ   Uh-huh.

SENATOR DIRKSEN   You've seen my amendments . . .

LBJ   . . . Just what I read in the paper . . .

SENATOR DIRKSEN (*surprised*)   I thought you were following this pretty closely?

LBJ   Naw, I think Humphrey's doin' a stand-up job as Floor Manager. You got any problems, you talk to Humphrey.

SENATOR DIRKSEN   Well, there are forty amendments I'm proposing . . .

LBJ   Forty! One for each year the children of Israel wandered in the desert? 'Course if old Moses spoke with your customary eloquence, the children of Israel probably woulda got to the Promised Land a whole lot sooner! You know everybody goes on and on about Reverend King's speechifyin' but he can't hold a candle to you!

SENATOR DIRKSEN (*modestly*)   No.

LBJ   I'm not just blowin' smoke up your ass, that's the God's truth, though you'll never read that in the *New York Times*.

SENATOR DIRKSEN (*flattered*)   Very kind of you, Mr. President.

LBJ   Humphrey is in awe of your speakin' ability. Green with envy. Forty amendments? Really? That many?

SENATOR DIRKSEN   My constituents have a number of concerns . . .

LBJ   Don't bullshit an old bullshitter, Everett. Let's cut to the chase here, shall we?

Dirksen smiles, thinking that finally a deal is at hand.

SENATOR DIRKSEN   Yes. Well, I think we have to strike Equal Employment all together. I can probably get my troops to accept Public Accommodations but with, say, a year of voluntary compliance before it becomes law.

LBJ   No.

SENATOR DIRKSEN   No?

LBJ   No.

SENATOR DIRKSEN   No?

LBJ   There an echo in here?

SENATOR DIRKSEN   The Southern filibuster cannot be defeated without substantial changes in the bill. I'm not promising anything, but if you are willing to compromise on your end, I think, I think I can deliver the necessary twenty-five Republican votes for cloture. Now it's your play. What do you have to say?

LBJ   No can do, Everett. Look, the bottom line is, either your people vote for the Bill, or you vote with the Segregationists and the country goes up in flames, and you get the hell beat out of you in November. We're making history here, Everett, and you've got to decide how you want history to remember you. As a Great Man, a man who changed the course of this country? Or just somebody who liked to hear himself talk.

LIGHTS SHIFT. Dirksen leaves as Humphrey enters excitedly.

SENATOR HUBERT HUMPHREY   Mr. President, Dirksen swallowed the "Great Man" hook and we have a deal! By the end of the day, most of his amendments boiled down to changing a comma here or there so the "Wizard of Ooze" could go back and tell the Republicans how tough he was.

LBJ shuffles through his all-important list of votes.

LBJ   You need 67 votes to invoke Cloture and stop the Filibuster. Do you have them?

SENATOR HUBERT HUMPHREY   We're very close, Mr. President.

LBJ   You're *two votes short!* We gotta find a way to undercut Russell's group, or get those last two goddamn votes!

SPOT out on Humphrey/SPOT ON Senator Russell on Senate floor. TB reads: **Day 68 of the Filibuster. 9:36 AM.**

SENATOR RUSSELL   Senator Dirksen's so-called amendments are like putting a band-aid on a cancer! I have an amendment to offer. I propose that we resettle Southern Negroes all over the country until racial proportions are equalized among the fifty states. I favor inflicting on New York and other cities the same conditions to be inflicted by this Bill on the innocent people of Georgia!

SPOT ON LBJ. TB reads: **Day 69 of the Filibuster. 3:51 PM.**

LBJ (*on phone*)   Senator Fulbright. I've got the name of this ole boy you've put down for the Federal Bench. Pretty tough sell for Humphrey's crowd but if you were to support the civil rights bill, they'd grin and bear it. Uh-huh, uh-huh, but maybe you don't have to fight quite as *hard* as you might otherwise?

SPOT OUT on LBJ/SPOT on **BYRD** *on Senate floor. TB reads:* **Day 71 of the Filibuster. 11:48 PM.**

SENATOR BYRD   Supporters of this Bill claim a scriptural basis in the commandment to "love thy neighbor" but I know my Bible and the Bible does not say that we may not choose our neighbor. The Bible does not say we can't build a wall betwixt us and our neighbor!

SPOT ON LBJ checking his list. TB reads: **Day 72 of the Filibuster. 1:05 PM.**

LBJ   WALTER!

Walter runs in.

Why the hell is Senator Engel of California suddenly off my list?

WALTER JENKINS   He's paralyzed with a malignant brain tumor, sir; recovering from surgery.

LBJ   Is he conscious?

WALTER JENKINS   I don't know, sir.

LBJ   Well, find out, goddamnit, if he's conscious, he can vote!

SPOT OUT on LBJ/Jenkins. SPOT on Senator Thurmond on Senate Floor. TB reads: **Day 73 of the Filibuster. 10:23 AM.**

SENATOR STROM THURMOND   This bill will guarantee the commercial destruction of white people everywhere! When it comes to employment, when it comes to promotion, when it comes to being laid off in times of economic distress, it ensures that the average garden variety American will have no choice whatsoever!

SPOT OUT on Thurmond. SPOT on LBJ. TB reads: **Day 74 of the Filibuster. 5:47 PM.**

LBJ (*on phone*)   Senator Hayden! For sixteen years, the thirsty citizens of Phoenix and Tucson have been waiting with the patience of Job for your Central Arizona Water Project. California's got the water and your people need it. You vote for cloture and I will personally see that water flowing and your deserts bloom. (*smiling*) Yessir. Uh-huh. You betcha.

SPOT OUT on LBJ/SPOT UP on Senator Eastland.TB reads: **6:12 PM**

SENATOR JIM EASTLAND   I am no anthropologist but I have studied History and there is no case in History of a mongrel race saving a civilization, much less creating one! This civil rights bill will take us back to Hitler, Stalin, and dictatorship!

SPOT OUT on Eastland/SPOT UP on LBJ.TB reads: **7:38 PM**

LBJ (*on phone*)   Senator Cannon! I got something here I think you're gonna want. *Water.* California water. Carl Hayden and I are finally puttin' together the Central Arizona Water Project and if Nevada wants any part of this, I need your vote. *Now.* Uh-huh. Thank you, Senator.

LBJ hangs up. Humphrey enters LBJ's SPOT.

Sixty-seven votes.

SENATOR HUBERT HUMPHREY   Yes, Mr. President, sixty-seven votes—we've beaten the filibuster! Should we let Senator Dirksen make the public announcement?

LBJ   Do you think there's any way we could stop him?

SPOT on Senator Dirksen and Press.

SENATOR DIRKSEN   Ladies and gentlemen, I am pleased to announce that we have reached agreement on a civil rights bill in the Senate. I am reminded of the great Victor Hugo who said, "Stronger than all the armies is an idea whose time has come." The time has come for equality of opportunity in sharing of government, in education, and in employment. It must not be stayed or denied.

TB reads: **June 19, 1964.** *SPOT on* **SPEAKER MANSFIELD**.

SENATOR MIKE MANSFIELD   The Senate may now vote on the Civil Rights Act of 1964!

Applause. SPOT on LBJ at desk surrounded by admirers, including MLK and Wilkins.

LBJ This Bill I sign today, the Civil Rights Act of 1964, is a further fulfilment of the ideals of the Declaration of Independence. I call on all Americans to help eliminate the last vestiges of discrimination in America. The Constitution, and the principles of freedom and morality, all forbid such unequal treatment—as will the law I sign today.

Applause as LBJ signs the bill and hands his pen to MLK.

Here you go, Dr. King.

MLK It's a great honor, Mr. President.

They shake hands. Actors on-stage freeze. LBJ turns to Russell.

LBJ I'm sorry, Dick.

SENATOR RUSSELL No, you're not.

LBJ It's not personal, Dick. It's just politics.

SENATOR RUSSELL I think I recall you tellin' Leland Olds somethin' like that, just after you cut his balls off with a rusty hacksaw.

A moment

It's the passin' of an era.

LBJ Yes it is.

SENATOR RUSSELL The passin' of a time of etiquette. Courtesy. The passin' of a time of principles, like Party unity.

LBJ (*smiling*) You know what the Old Soldier said when he was on parade? "Hey, look! Everybody's out of step but me."

SENATOR RUSSELL Maybe. I am old, and God knows I'm tired, but the fellas that are comin' up behind me are utterly without principles of any kind and you see how you like dealin' with them. You'll miss me when I'm gone.

LBJ I still need you, Dick.

SENATOR RUSSELL   I'm still here, Mr. President, but the rest of Dixie . . . ? I hope you haven't just killed your election chances.

Russell exits; LBJ watches him go. All actors exit. Humphrey crosses to LBJ.

SENATOR HUBERT HUMPHREY   Congratulations, Mr. President, on your glorious victory!

LBJ   The Democratic Party just lost the South for the rest of my lifetime and maybe yours. *(looking at Humphrey)* What the fuck are you so happy about?

LBJ walks off. LIGHTS DOWN.

END OF ACT ONE

ACT TWO

SPOT on LBJ.

LBJ *(to the audience)*   "Politics is war by other means." Bullshit. Politics is war. Period. Before Santa Anna stormed the Alamo his trumpeter played, "El Deguello"—it means, "I cut your throat." It means, no mercy. It means, no prisoners. That's a political campaign. Sometimes the battle is tens of thousands of people across dozens of states. And other times it's just you and him and it's a knife fight in a dark room with a slippery floor. There are no gracious losers and no sore losers; just the walking dead.

You know how you win a campaign? *By not losing it!* By spending every day as if it were your last day and you were ten points behind. By taking nothing for granted. By giving it everything you have and everything everybody around you has.

I only lost one election in my whole life. The son of a bitch stole it from me in the last seconds with a handful of fake votes and I will carry the pain of that with me to my dying day but I tell you what, nobody will ever do me that way again. It'll be some other way. The politician's curse, see, is the desperate desire, the absolute need to plan for every contingency, anticipate every problem, to control everything, even as you know that's impossible. You're not running for office; you're runnin' for your life. *You're trying to cheat death.*

SPOT out on LBJ.

TB reads: June 21, 1964. NESHOBA COUNTY, MISSISSIPPI. MIDNIGHT.

In the dark we hear a police siren start to wail, then the voices of three young men, **GOODMAN***,* **SCHWERNER***, and* **CHANEY***.*

SCHWERNER   Jesus! What does he want now?

GOODMAN   Are we over the speed limit?

71

SCHWERNER Hell, no.

CHANEY We weren't the first time he arrested us, either. This isn't right. What're you doin'? Don't *stop*, Mickey!

SCHWERNER It'll just give him an excuse to hold us!

CHANEY He don't need any fucking excuse! Get across the County line; it's the only place we'll be safe!

Sound of car as Schwerner stops. Sound of police cruiser pulling over. Sound of a car door. Sound of footsteps on gravel. Sound of **DEPUTY PRICE***.*

DEPUTY PRICE Out of the car, boys.

SCHWERNER What's the problem, Deputy Price? I thought we were good.

DEPUTY PRICE Outta the car, Jewboy.

A moment. Sound of three car doors closing.

LIGHTS UP on Oval Office. Walter, notes in hand, faces LBJ. As he names the victims, we see their images on the TB.

WALTER JENKINS Michael Schwerner, age 25; Andrew Goodman, age 21; and James Chaney, 21.

LBJ Twenty-one? Jesus, that's Lynda Bird's age.

WALTER JENKINS They were all working on the Freedom Summer Project in Meridian, Mississippi. Chaney is a local Negro but Schwerner and Goodman were both out-of-state volunteers. Both White.

LBJ picks up the phone.

LBJ White college kids; the shit'll hit the fan now. (*to Operator*) Get me the Governor of Mississippi.

TB reads: ***4 MONTHS TO THE ELECTION.***

WALTER JENKINS   They'd been investigating the burning of a Negro church in Neshoba County. They've been missing for fifteen hours now.

LBJ   Missing in Mississippi? They're dead. State authorities won't do shit in a case like this so King will be looking for me to pick up the slack but if I Federalize it, every Southern politician will be up in arms just as the Convention starts. Son of a bitch.

Phone Light blinks. LBJ picks up. SPOT on **MISSISSIPPI GOVERNOR JOHNSON** *eating pie and drinking a coke.*

Governor, I'm callin' 'bout those three boys . . .

GOVERNOR JOHNSON   . . . You mean those three professional agitators . . .

LBJ   . . . Chaney, Schwerner, and Goodman . . . .

GOVERNOR JOHNSON   . . . that come into our state creatin' all kinds of problems.

LBJ   I know. I know. We got the NAACP outside picketin' the White House as we speak. Listen, 'bout these boys who went missin' yesterday in Neshoba county. (*glancing at Walter's notes*) Apparently, a Deputy Price arrested them yesterday afternoon . . .

GOVERNOR JOHNSON   . . . drivin' thirty-five miles over the speed limit . . .

LBJ   . . . Really?

GOVERNOR JOHNSON   Yes, sir. So they held them for a couple of hours . . .

LBJ   . . . Well, that's confusing, see, 'cause when their friends called the jail down there, the Deputy said he'd never heard of 'em.

GOVERNOR JOHNSON   I don't know anything about that. Price says he released them about 10:00 that night . . .

LBJ   . . . and nobody's heard from them since.

GOVERNOR JOHNSON   Well, I think it's a publicity stunt! These boys are hiding somewhere, probably havin' themselves a good laugh, and then they're gonna come out and claim they been abused or somethin'. Could be in Cuba right now, for all we know.

LBJ   Well, as you can imagine their parents are real worried.

Governor says nothing. Furious, LBJ picks up the phone.

Now, I would hate to have to send a buncha Federal Marshals into your state . . .

GOVERNOR JOHNSON (*suddenly concerned*)   . . . No. No, you don't want to do that . . .

LBJ   . . . 'Course I don't! You don't want the publicity and I sure don't want to stir up a mess with just eight weeks before the Democratic Convention but there's a lotta pressure to do *something*. If you'd rather, I guess I could get a few FBI agents to look into the thing.

GOVERNOR JOHNSON   FBI?

LBJ   Well, that's a damn sight better than Federal Marshals and the US Army, isn't it?

GOVERNOR JOHNSON   Well, yeah; I guess so.

LBJ   I think you got the right idea, Governor; let this be Hoover's problem, not ours. Hopefully, you're right about the whole thing and these boys'll turn up quick and we can all relax. Christ sakes, we got an election to win!

LBJ hangs up. SPOT out on Gov. Johnson.

WALTER JENKINS   Hoover will just drag his feet.

LBJ   Not if I light a fire under his ass.

LBJ punches another number. SPOT on Hoover.

J. EDGAR HOOVER   Mr. President?

LBJ Jay, the Governor of Mississippi wants the FBI to look into these missin' kids.

J. EDGAR HOOVER Well, I'd be happy to, Mr. President, but there's a jurisdictional problem . . .

LBJ . . . No, no, I talked to Bobby about that and he says we got the Lindbergh Statute on our side . . .

J. EDGAR HOOVER . . . Mr. President, we don't have the resources down there and . . .

LBJ . . . Yeah, I never understood how come you don't have an actual Office in Mississippi.

J. EDGAR HOOVER Well, frankly, there's not a lot of need down there.

LBJ I'm not gonna tell you how to run your shop but the problem here is, the governor asked *specifically* for the FBI to investigate. I tried to put him off but I suppose I could get some other third party. I know Senator Jim Eastland wants Alan Dulles investigatin'.

J. EDGAR HOOVER *Dulles?*

LBJ His experience in the CIA and all would probably be a very . . .

J. EDGAR HOOVER . . . Oh, no, Mr. President, no, I don't think that's a good idea! This is very clearly an FBI matter.

LBJ Well, if you're sure. I mean, the last thing I'd want is Dulles down there actin' like he was runnin' the FBI! Tell you what, let's say Eastland is my problem; I'll deal with him. You get your agents down there to Neshoba County and wrap this thing up quick.

J. EDGAR HOOVER Yes, sir, Mr. President.

SPOT out on Hoover. LBJ hangs up and smiles conspiratorially at Walter.

WALTER JENKINS When did you talk to Eastland about Dulles going down there?

LBJ I made that part up. Hoover hates Dulles, ever since he got the top job at the CIA and Hoover didn't. We might still send Dulles down there, just to keep Hoover working hard. The problem here is, there's three sovereignties involved: there's the United States, there's the state of Mississippi, and then there's J. Edgar Hoover.

LIGHTS out on Oval Office. LIGHTS up on hotel room. MLK confers with Stokely, Abernathy, Moses, and Wilkins.

STOKELY CARMICHAEL They're goddamn liars! ALL OF THEM! Bob and I talked to that Sheriff Rainey and Deputy Price and they just nodded and smirked and the whole time you could tell they were just laughing at us.

MLK We have to assume those young men are dead.

ROY WILKINS There were no bodies in the car they found.

STOKELY CARMICHAEL Oh, well, they're probably on vacation then. I always set my car on fire before I take a weekend off. They were *murdered*, and I wanta know, where's the goddamn government?

ROY WILKINS The President has sent the FBI in to investigate.

STOKELY CARMICHAEL *Before.* Where was the government *before?*

BOB MOSES We asked the Justice Department for protection before we even started Freedom Summer.

STOKELY CARMICHAEL Begged for it but they said no. Now two *White* kids get disappeared and suddenly the FBI is magically there!

MLK I will ask the President to provide protection for your remaining staff and forcefully press the case against Sheriff Rainey and his bunch.

RALPH ABERNATHY It's the least they can do now.

ROY WILKINS I warned you, you were sending people to their death. Freedom Summer is over. SNCC has got to get everybody out of there before somebody else gets killed. *Now.*

BOB MOSES That's the message you want to send? Kill one of us and we'll all run away?

STOKELY CARMICHAEL We're not goin' anywhere!

ROY WILKINS Let me ask you something, you been there two months and how many voters have you actually registered?

Bob and Stokely glance at one another.

STOKELY CARMICHAEL Twelve hundred; give or take.

ROY WILKINS That's all?!

BOB MOSES This is *Mississippi,* Roy.

STOKELY CARMICHAEL And people who don't have the balls to put themselves on the line of fire got no right to criticize.

ROY WILKINS Three people killed so far, maybe more. Five hundred beaten or arrested. Thirty-five churches burned. Thirty Negro homes and businesses dynamited. For twelve hundred votes?

BOB MOSES It's not just the votes. For the first time, Black people are building a new political party . . .

ROY WILKINS . . . "The Mississippi Freedom Democratic Party." I heard. More Bob Moses pie in the sky. Martin . . .

STOKELY CARMICHAEL . . . Hey, we tried to play by the rules and integrate the regular Democratic Party and they kept us out. Fine. We build our own Democratic Party but with a difference.

BOB MOSES Open to *everybody,* white or black.

RALPH ABERNATHY Roy, don't you think America ought to have at least one political party that isn't racist?

STOKELY CARMICHAEL Wouldn't that be something?

ROY WILKINS It's a waste of time! You, what, send 'em to the Democratic Convention in Atlantic City and march around the parking lot with cardboard signs singing, "We Shall Overcome"?

BOB MOSES   Hell no. Not after what happened to Goodman, Chaney, and Schwerner. Yeah, we send our delegates to the Convention—where they challenge the legality of the segregated Mississippi delegation on National TV and *dare LBJ not to seat us.*

Stunned silence.

ROY WILKINS   You are children playing with dynamite. Lyndon Johnson may wipe his snotty nose on his sleeve redneck style but he is the best President the Negro has had since Abraham Lincoln. If you challenge LBJ at the convention, at the very least, you will embarrass him, and this man has a long memory for those who've crossed him. In the worst case, you cost him votes and he loses the election to Barry Fucking Goldwater! (*turns on King*) Are you so desperate to have their approval, Martin, that you would sanction this mass suicide?

MLK   Roy, those three young men went to Mississippi and died doing the work the government has not been willing to do for a hundred years. *We have to take a stand.*

ROY WILKINS   I grieve for those young men. Don't use their funeral pyre to burn what's left of the Movement.

Wilkins leaves the room.

MLK   How can I help, Bob?

BOB MOSES   Come to Mississippi.

RALPH ABERNATHY   Don't be ridiculous!

BOB MOSES   Show the people you're behind the Mississippi Freedom Democratic Party.

RALPH ABERNATHY   You might just as well paint a target on his back and declare Open Season!

STOKELY CARMICHAEL (*ignoring Abernathy*)   You haven't been to Mississippi in over a year . . .

RALPH ABERNATHY . . . He's been busy! Death threats. Jail. *Shot at!* You don't have any monopoly on suffering here, Stokely. Let somebody else carry this load, Martin. Please.

A moment.

MLK Of course I'll come.

LIGHTS down on MLK/Others. LIGHTS up on FBI Agents digging for the remains of the missing civil rights workers. The smell is awful and the Agents smoke cigars to keep the stench down. Simultaneously, LIGHTS up on LBJ and Humphrey in Oval Office. Both men are tense; nervous. Jenkins is delivering the latest FBI report. TB reads: 3 MONTHS TO THE ELECTION.

WALTER JENKINS The FBI was acting on a tip about a farm in rural Mississippi and they've just found two bodies buried there in an earthen dam.

LBJ Jesus. They're sure it's them?

WALTER JENKINS They found Schwerner's draft card in his back pocket.

LBJ My God.

WALTER JENKINS Goodman's body was right below his. It appears they'd both been shot once in the chest. They're still digging for Chaney.

LBJ (*shaking his head*) The minute McNamara arrives—send him in.

LBJ waves and Jenkins leaves.

It's clear that Deputy Price is involved, probably the Sheriff, too.

SENATOR HUBERT HUMPHREY Will the State authorities bring charges?

LBJ In Mississippi? Don't be stupid. The whole mess is in my lap now. If I don't charge those bastards then King yells I'm lettin' them get away with murder but if I do charge 'em then all the

Southerners scream about how I'm taking orders from the nigras and all two weeks before the start of the goddamn Convention!

SENATOR HUBERT HUMPHREY   I'm sorry to have to tell you, Mr. President, but word is that Governor Wallace offered himself to Goldwater as the Republican Vice Presidential candidate.

LBJ   That little weasel would sell his own mother to get a leg up.

SENATOR HUBERT HUMPHREY   Goldwater passed.

LBJ   Maybe Goldwater's not as stupid as he looks.

SENATOR HUBERT HUMPHREY   But Strom Thurmond is formally switching parties.

LBJ   Mother-fucking traitor. The question is, is anybody else gonna follow him out the door?

SENATOR HUBERT HUMPHREY   I don't know.

LBJ (*switching gears*)   Well find out! And when are you gonna get my damn Poverty Bill outta Committee?

SENATOR HUBERT HUMPHREY   They're taking a very tough stand.

LBJ   That Bill will help poor people in their own states but the bastards don't care, they just wanta cut my balls off before the election. (*beat*) You see her on TV?

SENATOR HUBERT HUMPHREY   Who?

LBJ   The dead kid's wife. Schwerner.

SENATOR HUBERT HUMPHREY   Rita.

LBJ   Widow, I mean. Christ. You see this? King sent me another telegram this morning, wants me to send more Federal Marshals to Mississippi to protect the remaining civil rights workers.

SENATOR HUBERT HUMPHREY   Will you?

LBJ   What choice do I have? Another murder and there'll be a race riot.

McNamara enters, very tense, carrying a red briefing folder.

ROBERT MCNAMARA Mr. President, we have word . . .

McNamara hesitates when he sees Humphrey.

LBJ Go ahead.

ROBERT MCNAMARA Captain Herrick of the *USS Maddox* reports a potential sighting last night of two possibly hostile unidentified vessels in the Gulf of Tonkin.

LBJ Uh huh.

ROBERT MCNAMARA And some somewhat contradictory sonar evidence of actual torpedo attack.

LBJ A "potential" sighting? What the hell is a potential sighting?

ROBERT MCNAMARA A visual sighting not confirmed by mechanical means.

LBJ And this torpedo attack actually happened?

ROBERT MCNAMARA Still awaiting confirmation.

LBJ Were any of our ships hit?

ROBERT MCNAMARA No, sir.

LBJ Any explosions?

ROBERT MCNAMARA No, sir.

LBJ (*exasperated*) Then how the hell do we know we were attacked?

ROBERT MCNAMARA We don't, for sure. We have contradictory sonar readings.

LBJ For Christ's sake, Robert, give me something to work with here!

ROBERT MCNAMARA The weather is very bad right now, Mr. President; squalls; fifteen foot swells; no moon. It's not like the attack two days ago.

SENATOR HUBERT HUMPHREY   We were attacked two days ago?

LBJ   We've been trying to keep a lid on this for obvious reasons not the least of which is we were in North Vietnam's waters, playin' around up there.

SENATOR HUBERT HUMPHREY   Some kind of clandestine raids?

LBJ   Another one of Kennedy's plans. Not mine. I didn't start any of this but it's damn sure my problem now.

ROBERT MCNAMARA (*warning look to LBJ*)   Officially, this is a very delicate subject.

LBJ   Humphrey can know! So, we were up there, messing around, and they came out with their PT Boats to give us a warning, and we knocked the hell outta 'em.

SENATOR HUBERT HUMPHREY   Why are we back there?

ROBERT MCNAMARA   We're not back there, we're in International Waters this time.

SENATOR HUBERT HUMPHREY   But close?

ROBERT MCNAMARA   *International waters.* We have drawn a line and dared them to cross it. It appears they have. (*to LBJ*) Mr. President, the limited air strikes that you ordered pre-selected in case of another attack are good to go.

SENATOR HUBERT HUMPHREY   Air strikes?

ROBERT MCNAMARA   Shall we order them in?

SENATOR HUBERT HUMPHREY   Surely this is a situation about which we ought to be more confident before we act!

ROBERT MCNAMARA   There is no sense pretending that last night's event didn't happen. Not anymore.

LBJ rises, coldly furious.

LBJ   What do you mean?

ROBERT MCNAMARA   There has been a leak somewhere and the press . . .

LBJ   . . . Who? Who leaked it?

ROBERT MCNAMARA   We're tracking it down.

LBJ   I want his fucking head in a basket!

ROBERT MCNAMARA   The point is, the press has got to it somehow and now there are domestic considerations as well.

SENATOR HUBERT HUMPHREY   Such as?

LBJ   Goldwater.

ROBERT MCNAMARA   If you don't retaliate, you know he will play all the angles against you.

LBJ   The whole "soft on the military" bullshit. Christ, Democrats beat Hitler and Tojo, what more do we have to do?

ROBERT MCNAMARA   Do you want me to call in the retaliatory strikes?

SENATOR HUBERT HUMPHREY   For an attack which may or may not have happened?!

ROBERT MCNAMARA   The planes are ready to go on your command.

SENATOR HUBERT HUMPHREY   This puts the President in a, uh, it puts *you*, Mr. President, in a terrible position. You are essentially going to have to, to . . .

ROBERT MCNAMARA   . . . Mr. President . . . !

SENATOR HUBERT HUMPHREY   . . . to lie!

A Moment.

LBJ   Do it.

McNamara leaves. Simultaneously, the FBI Agents slowly lift a clay-covered body—Chaney—out of the grave.

ROBERT MCNAMARA Yes, sir.

SENATOR HUBERT HUMPHREY What if it comes out?

LBJ We'll pass it off on our South Vietnamese allies.

SENATOR HUBERT HUMPHREY Mr. President . . .

LBJ You think I like this? Puttin' my ass in a sling just before the election when those dumb stupid sailors are maybe just shootin' at, I don't know what, flyin' fish, maybe?

SENATOR HUBERT HUMPHREY I don't know but I certainly . . .

LBJ . . . Maybe you think Goldwater should be President! Is that it?

SENATOR HUBERT HUMPHREY I never said that!

LBJ That maniac wants to lob an A-bomb into the Kremlin's bathroom and start World War Three! You see how you like that.

SENATOR HUBERT HUMPHREY Mr. President, come on now.

LBJ Goldwater gets elected, you can forget about poverty; you can forget about civil rights. Is that what you want? I'm tryin' to turn this country around and prevent a major war. Christ, why the hell did I ever consider you for my Vice President? At the first sign of trouble you cut and run!

SENATOR HUBERT HUMPHREY I'm not running anywhere; I'm standing right here, beside you!

LBJ Precious cold comfort you are. (*a moment*) Congress will back me on this. An election year? I'll get 'em to pass some kind of resolution, authorize me full authority over there, and then *we can get back to the things that really matter.*

Walter enters.

WALTER JENKINS Sir, they've found Chaney's body.

LIGHTS DOWN on LBJ/Humphrey. Blast of Choir music as LIGHTS UP on Union Baptist Church, Meridian, Miss. Choir finishes the hymn as Chaney's body is carried in and set down in his coffin.

MLK   James Chaney gave his life to make this country live up to its forgotten promises and unfulfilled ideals. We all know the dark and savage history of Mississippi. We all know the terror and the violence you have endured here. We all know the terrible sadness that you feel today in your hearts. But we will not live in despair. We will not surrender. We will continue to respond to their violence with love and forgiveness and our struggle will succeed because you ...

DAVID DENNIS, *CORE leader in Mississippi interrupts.*

DAVID DENNIS   ...As I stand here, I not only blame the people who pulled the trigger or did the beating or dug the hole with a shovel, I blame the State of Mississippi on up to the people in Washington, D.C., for what happened! You know what I'm sayin'?

CONGREGANT #1 (*quiet admonishment*)   That's enough of that.

MLK   No, it's alright.

DAVID DENNIS   I'm sick and tired of going to funerals for black men who have been murdered by white men.

CROWD   AMEN/That's right/Tell it.

DAVID DENNIS   Are you? Are you sick and tired of this stuff like I am?

CROWD   Yessir!/Uh-huh!/That's right!

DAVID DENNIS   I'm not feeling sad tonight, Dr. King. I'm not feeling sorrowful. I'm not feeling *forgiveness*. I've got—I've got vengeance in my heart and I ask you to feel angry with me. Are you angry? Are you? You feel what I'm feeling in my heart? Cause I'm feeling VENGEANCE in my heart!

CROWD   YES!

85

MLK watches with growing concern as the audience responds to Dennis's anger with their own calls for retaliation.

DAVID DENNIS   The white men who murdered James Chaney are never going to be punished!

CROWD   NO!/THAT'S WRONG!/NO!

DAVID DENNIS   I ask you to be sick and tired of that. I'm tired of people in this country allowing that to continue to happen. We've got to stand up.

CROWD   STAND UP!/Yeah!/That's right!/Stand up!

DAVID DENNIS   We got to stand up! The best way to remember James Chaney is to demand our rights. You hear me? DEMAND our rights! Don't just look at me and go back and tell folks you've been to a nice service. Your work is just beginning. If you go back home and sit down and take what these white men in Mississippi are doing to us. If you take it and don't do something about it—then GOD DAMN YOUR SOULS! STAND UP!

CROWD   STAND UP!

DAVID DENNIS   WE GOT TO STAND UP IN MERIDIAN!

CROWD   STAND UP!

DAVID DENNIS   WE GOT TO STAND UP IN JACKSON!

CROWD   STAND UP!

DAVID DENNIS   *AND WHEN WE GET TO ATLANTIC CITY, WHAT'RE WE GONNA DO?*

CROWD   STAND UP!

DAVID DENNIS   WHAT'RE WE GONNA DO?!

CROWD   STAND UP!

DAVID DENNIS/CROWD   STAND UP! STAND UP! STAND UP! STAND UP!

As MLK walks DS into a SPOT, the TB suddenly explodes in garish neon and sparkling lights announcing: **ATLANTIC CITY WELCOMES THE NATIONAL DEMOCRATIC CONVENTION!**

The Mourners morph into black **MFDP ACTIVISTS** *outside the Convention center, carrying signs, passing out leaflets reading "Seat the MFDP," and chanting. They freeze as Humphrey joins MLK for a private conversation.*

TB reads: **76 DAYS TO THE ELECTION.**

MLK   The Convention *has got* to seat our delegates!

SENATOR HUBERT HUMPHREY   It's not that simple, Martin.

MLK   *Yes, it is!* You don't understand the depth of feeling out there. There are serious divisions growing in the Movement and if my people decide that non-violence is worthless, I will not be able to control them. It may already be too late.

SPOT OUT on MLK/Humphrey.

MFDP LEADER   Support the MFDP!

MFDP ACTIVISTS   Support the MFDP!

MFDP LEADER   Seat our delegates!

MFDP ACTIVISTS   Seat our delegates!

MFDP LEADER   Seat them now!

MFDP ACTIVISTS   Seat them now!

SOUND of recorded version of "Hello Lyndon" begins playing as **WHITE DEMOCRATIC DELEGATES** *begin entering the Convention Hall. The Activists descend on the Delegates, pressing leaflets into their hands and button-holing them.*

A **NETWORK CORRESPONDENT** *appears, mike in hand.*

NETWORK CORRESPONDENT   The Democratic Convention officially starts tomorrow but the fireworks have already begun! While President Johnson waits in the White House until the last night of the Convention, when he formally accepts the nomination, tension is building to a fever pitch. Who will his Vice Presidential candidate be? Robert Kennedy? Senator Humphrey? Or someone else?

MFDP LEADER   Support the MFDP!

MFDP ACTIVISTS   Support the MFDP!

NETWORK CORRESPONDENT   But the big question is, will the Democratic Party seat the so-called "Mississippi Freedom" Delegates in place of the regular Mississippi Delegates?!

All sound cuts out. Everyone leaves the stage except LBJ and Walter in the Oval Office. LBJ slams the phone down just as Humphrey enters.

SENATOR HUBERT HUMPHREY   You have to seat them, Mr. President.

LBJ   John Connelly, the Governor of my own state, just told me, "If you seat those black buggers, not only will Texas quit, but the whole South will walk out!" My own people turning their backs on me. How is that gonna look on National TV?

Walter enters. Hesitates . . .

What?

WALTER JENKINS   The ballot in Alabama, sir—apparently Governor Wallace has kept your name off it.

LBJ   That little piece of shit.

SENATOR HUBERT HUMPHREY   Can he do that?

LBJ   'Course he can! Goldwater must be laughin' his ass off. We have got to hold the South and this mess with the Mississippi delegates is the key. Eastland and his bunch are insistin' they are the true Democratic party when they won't even say they will support me and now they're threatenin' to walk out of the convention!

Lady Bird enters with a sandwich on a plate which she puts in front of LBJ.

LADY BIRD JOHNSON   Lyndon? Why don't you take a break from all this, honey . . .

LBJ   I'm fine, Bird.

LADY BIRD JOHNSON   Well, you certainly don't sound fine. When's the last time you ate anything?

LBJ   Go away, Bird, you're givin' me a goddamn headache.

LADY BIRD JOHNSON   Oh, honey, I'm just worried . . .

LBJ   LEAVE ME ALONE! GET THE HELL OUTTA HERE! GO ON!

Lady Bird hurries out. Walter discretely follows her. Lady Bird pauses in hallway stifling her tears. Walter offers her his handkerchief. She wipes her face fiercely.

LADY BIRD JOHNSON   I just feel so sorry for him.

WALTER JENKINS   I know.

LADY BIRD JOHNSON   They're all being so mean.

WALTER JENKINS   It's not fair.

LADY BIRD JOHNSON   Thank God he has you, Walter.

WALTER JENKINS   And you.

Lady Bird fixes her lipstick.

LADY BIRD JOHNSON   People think he's hard on me; well, he's hard on everybody; especially himself. People don't see that; I do. I see it *all*. His—lady friends. I'm the one he chose and at the end of the day, I'm the one he comes home to. My money paid for his first campaign, did you know that? Had to face down my own daddy over my inheritance to get it—and by God, it was the best investment I ever made. My lipstick OK?

WALTER JENKINS You look beautiful.

LADY BIRD JOHNSON No, I'm not, but you make do with what you got and whatever happens you don't quit.

MFDP LEADER Seat the MFDP!

MFDP ACTIVISTS Seat the MFDP!

As Lady Bird straightens her back and exits, another AIDE hands Walter a Telegram which he quickly carries back into the Oval Office, glancing at it as he does so.

WALTER JENKINS Sir? Another telegram from Dr. King . . .

MFDP LEADER Seat them now!

MFDP ACTIVISTS Seat them now!

LBJ snatches it out of Walter's hand and reads it.

LBJ Now he publicly *"demands"* that I support the MFDP. Goddamn it, what do King and these people want? I got a civil rights bill passed and I'm workin' on a Poverty bill that will do more for them than any bullshit symbolic vote could ever hope to achieve but do they thank me for it? No. King says that come November, Black Voters might sit on their hands!

SENATOR HUBERT HUMPHREY He actually said that?

LBJ That's what he means! Sometimes I don't wonder if Hoover isn't right about King; maybe the Communists have got a hold of him.

SENATOR HUBERT HUMPHREY Look, I spoke to Dr. King personally and he's genuinely worried that after those murders there will be a rising tide of *anger* in the Negro community that can't be controlled by anybody.

LBJ So now he's threatening me with riots, too?

SENATOR HUBERT HUMPHREY That's not what he means . . .

LBJ   To hell with'em! Let'em all vote for Goldwater!

SENATOR HUBERT HUMPHREY   You don't mean that.

LBJ   Even as we speak, Republican groups nationwide are purging their membership of Negroes but hey, if *I'm* so bad, then join Barry's little Nazi party! Just a little—respect. Love. Is that too much to ask for? Shit.

SENATOR HUBERT HUMPHREY   Mr. President. What do you want to do?

LBJ   You have to make them compromise.

SENATOR HUBERT HUMPHREY   Me?

LBJ   Hell, yes, you, you're the big Liberal leader in the Senate. Everybody . . . .

LBJ	**SENATOR HUBERT HUMPHREY**
. . . likes you.	. . . likes me.

LBJ   You go down there and frankly, I don't care what you do or how you do it, but you find me a compromise and keep the South from walkin' out or *you will never be my Vice President.* You hear me? (*re: the TV*) Who the hell is that testifying to the Credentials Committee?

Humphrey turns up the sound on the TV.

SPOT on **FANNIE LOU HAMER** *as she talks to the Committee on live television about her experiences in Mississippi. Simultaneously, a live streaming of her image on the TB.*

SENATOR HUBERT HUMPHREY   Fannie Lou Hamer. She's one of the leaders of the MFDP.

FANNIE LOU HAMER   On June 9, 1963, I went to a meetin' to learn how to register Negro voters in Mississippi. On my way back, I was arrested by the Winona police Chief and taken to County Jail.

LBJ   My God.

91

FANNIE LOU HAMER   After I was placed in the cell, a State Highway Patrolman ordered me to lie facedown on the bunk bed saying, "You are goin' to wish you were dead."

SENATOR HUBERT HUMPHREY   This is awful.

LBJ   It sure as hell is.

FANNIE LOU HAMER   And then he ordered two male Negro prisoners to beat me with a blackjack.

Fannie takes a drink of water.

LBJ   She could stampede the Liberals into seating the MFDP and the South will storm outta the Convention in droves. We gotta stop this right now. Walter! Tell the press the President has an important announcement to make in the Rose Garden. Right now!

Walter runs out.

SENATOR HUBERT HUMPHREY   What announcement?

LBJ   Hell, if I know. Anythin' to turn those damn cameras off in Atlantic City!

LIGHTS down on LBJ/Humphrey.

FANNIE LOU HAMER   And the first prisoner beat me till he was exhausted and then the Patrolman ordered the second Negro to beat me and I began to work my feet, and the Patrolman ordered the first Negro who beat me to set on my feet to keep me from working my feet. I began to scream and one white man began to beat me in my head and tell me to hush. My dress had worked up high and I pulled it down and this other white man, he walked over and pulled my dress back up. All this on account we want to register to vote, to become first class citizens. And if the Freedom Democratic Party is not seated at this convention, I question America. Is this America, the land of the free and the home of the brave, where our lives be threatened daily because we want to live as decent human beings in America . . . ?

Static crosses TB. Fannie looks confused.

What? I don't understand?

Fannie's face on TB is replaced by **NETWORK CORRESPONDENT**.

NETWORK CORRESPONDENT We interrupt this regularly scheduled broadcast to bring you a special announcement from the President of the United States. We take you now to the Rose Garden at the White House.

LBJ appears before PRESS in the Rose Garden. Simultaneously, his face is broadcast. Image fills the TB.

LBJ Howdy. I wanta thank y'all for showing up on such short notice. I know a lot of people are still wonderin' who my Vice Presidential candidate will be and I will be makin' my choice very soon, I promise, but a, a lot of thought has to go into a decision like that.

LIGHTS SHIFT. LBJ steps away from the podium and pulls Hoover aside.

I need to know everything King and that Fannie Lou Person and Bob Moses and all those MFDP delegates are talking about! I want them under constant surveillance, the whole bunch of them!

J. EDGAR HOOVER Mr. President, we don't have any warrant or . . .

LBJ . . . That never stopped you before, did it?! I don't care what you do and I don't care how you do it, in fact it's better if I don't know, but everything you get, you send it immediately to Walter.

WALTER JENKINS Mr. President? Senator Jim Eastland on Line One.

LBJ leaves. Hoover is shaken.

J. EDGAR HOOVER (*quietly*) Lyndon is way out of line here. There's not a shred of legal justification for this; he's using the Bureau for pure political advantage.

DEKE DELOACH   What do you want to do?

Hoover considers carefully, then . . .

J. EDGAR HOOVER   He's the President. Give him what he wants, of course.

LIGHTS down on Hoover/Deloach. SPOT on LBJ in Oval Office on phone. SPOT on Senator Eastland on phone.

SENATOR JIM EASTLAND   This whole thing has gotten outta hand now!

LBJ   Well, you got no one to blame but yourself, Senator Eastland. Have the Mississippi Regulars come to this convention as traitors to the Party, or are they gonna support the nominee?

SENATOR JIM EASTLAND   "Traitors to the Party"? Lotta my folks feel like Strom Thurmond and George Wallace, that the Democratic Party is pushin' them out.

LBJ   Oh, come on, we both know how those delegates of yours were selected. Not a black face in the bunch. How's that gonna look on National Television?

SENATOR JIM EASTLAND   How's it gonna look when all those good white folks you so easily disparage walk out?

LBJ   *You threatenin' me?*

SENATOR JIM EASTLAND   I'm just sayin' feelin's are runnin' high . . .

LBJ   . . . look, at the end of the day, we all got to find us some kind of compromise here.

SENATOR JIM EASTLAND   I don't know. Those MFDP people are just backwoods people, you can't reason with them.

LBJ   Well, here's what I'm thinkin'. They can be seated in the Convention . . . (*over Eastland's objections*) . . . but *they don't get a vote*, alright, no actual vote. In return, the Regular delegates, your people, sign a Loyalty Oath to support the nominee.

SENATOR JIM EASTLAND A Loyalty Oath? What kinda Socialist crap is that?

LBJ Just a public statement of *intention* to support the nominee would do, even if they knew they were gonna support Goldwater.

SENATOR JIM EASTLAND To be perfectly frank, Mr. President, the Mississippi Party nearly endorsed Goldwater already.

LBJ Is that so?

SENATOR JIM EASTLAND I'm just sayin'.

LBJ Boy howdie, poor ole Mississippi is making it impossible for me to help my friends. You know, Jim, I get grief all the time from Northern liberals sayin', "How come we gotta pay Mississippi farmers NOT to plant?" Mebbe they're right. Since I'm not gonna carry Mississippi anyway maybe I oughta cut your goddamn six million dollar cotton subsidies! How much of that do you receive on your plantation down there in Sunflower County?

SENATOR JIM EASTLAND Hold on, hold on ...

LBJ *I'm just sayin'.*

SENATOR JIM EASTLAND Tell you what, lemme talk to the delegates, see what I can do.

LBJ You do that. And get back to me with some good news. *Soon.* (*LBJ hangs up*) Walter! I need to talk to Uncle Dick but first get me Wallace on the phone. Time to deal with that pissant.

SPOT DOWN on LBJ/Walter/Eastland.

SPOT UP on Wallace and his aide, **TRAMMEL**. *Governor's Mansion, Alabama ...*

GOVERNOR GEORGE WALLACE What did Goldwater say about his visit to Alabama? Did you tell him what I can do for him here?

SEYMORE TRAMMEL (*pained*) He said, well, I was told quite firmly, that Goldwater would prefer you to be out of the state when he arrives.

GOVERNOR GEORGE WALLACE   Son of a bitch. Goddamn son of a bitch.

SEYMORE TRAMMEL   It's just politics, George.

GOVERNOR GEORGE WALLACE   You think I don't know that?! You think I don't understand "Politics!" When he wanted me to drop outta the race, butter wouldn't melt in his mouth, but as soon as I did, he rolled me over and threw my clothes at me like I was a fifty-cent whore and he couldn't wait to wash my stink off. He's not the first to underestimate me. By God!

A flustered Lurleen runs in.

LURLEEN WALLACE   George! It's the President on the phone!

Wallace smiles at Trammel.

GOVERNOR GEORGE WALLACE   Guess the mountain has come to Mohammed.

SPOT on LBJ.

Mr. President. How's your big party up there in Atlantic City?

LBJ   Cut the crap, George. How come my name isn't on the voting ballot in Alabama? Apparently the only names on there are Goldwater supporters and folks committed to your candidacy which you ended a month ago.

GOVERNOR GEORGE WALLACE   Well, Mr. President, that's just one of those unfortunate things. An error in the registrar's office.

LBJ   Then you need to fix that.

GOVERNOR GEORGE WALLACE   I wish I could but I can't.

LBJ   You tellin' me that you don't have control of your own state bureaucracy? Way I hear it, from Mobile County to Jackson County can't a mule fart without your permission.

GOVERNOR GEORGE WALLACE (*enjoying himself*)   Now, Mr. President, you're gettin' me all mixed up with the Lord, and sparrows falling, and whatnot.

LBJ   If you think helpin' to elect a whole buncha Republican legislators in Alabama is gonna help you, you musta got knocked around in the ring too much in your boxing days when you was a chicken weight.

GOVERNOR GEORGE WALLACE   *Bantam.* I was a bantam weight.

LBJ   Don't seem to me that Goldwater is acting all that grateful to you, is he? Turned you down flat is what I hear and won't even be seen in public with you. Now, look, we had our differences, you got in some good licks but you lost and it's time to put that aside. Come November 4th there's only gonna be one winner and you're gonna want to be on my team. I know your people pride themselves on their long memory but I'm gonna tell you somethin', George, it ain't nothin' to *my* memory. I don't ever forget.

GOVERNOR GEORGE WALLACE   Like an elephant, you mean?

LBJ   I mean, "Governor," that in one more year your term is up and under Alabama law, you can't run for a third term. Who's gonna have you, George? Not the Party of Lincoln; Goldwater made that clear. Not any of those Democrats you screwed over. Whatcha gonna do?

LIGHTS out on George/Lurleen/Trammel. LBJ hangs up and turns to Jenkins.

I think he actually enjoys being the turd in the crystal punch bowl.

WALTER JENKINS   I have Senator Russell for you on Two.

LBJ picks up the phone and punches a button.

LBJ   Uncle Dick.

SPOT up on Senator Russell on phone.

SENATOR RUSSELL   You're up awful late, Mr. President.

97

LBJ   They're all ganging up on me, Dick.

SENATOR RUSSELL   You're gonna give yourself another heart attack.

LBJ   Well, if I do, it'll be George Wallace and Martin Luther King puts me in my grave. You hear about this public telegram of King's *demanding* I seat the MFDP? The whole country will think that Negroes have more power in the Democratic Party than the President has and the whole South will bolt!

SENATOR RUSSELL   I warned you about that.

LBJ (*confiding*)   I tell you what I really think. I think this is somethin' King cooked up with Bobby Kennedy to embarrass me. Kennedy is trying to stab me in the back and steal the nomination at the last minute.

SENATOR RUSSELL   Mr. President, Robert Kennedy has no interest, whatsoever, in hurtin' you or helpin' Barry Goldwater.

LBJ   To hell with'em all. I'm gonna go back to my ranch and the people who love me. I never wanted to be President in the first place!

SENATOR RUSSELL (*irritated*)   Mr. President, forgive my frankness, but you are speakin' like a child, and a spoiled child at that! You and I both know you're not serious. Now take a tranquilizer and get yourself some sleep!

Russell hangs up. SPOT down on Russell.

LBJ   He hung up on me. The son of a bitch hung up on me!

SPOT down on LBJ. SPOT on MLK.

MLK   Dear Mr. President. STOP. Why does seating the Mississippi Freedom Party matter so much? STOP. For all the disenfranchised millions of this earth, those in Mississippi and Alabama, or behind the Iron Curtain or suffering the Apartheid of South Africa— recognition of the Freedom Party would say to them that, yes, somewhere in this world there is a nation that cares about justice!

STOP. Conscience demands that you publicly join us in seating the Freedom Party delegates! STOP. Yours sincerely, Dr. Martin Luther King. STOP.

SPOT UP on Pageant Hotel Room, Atlantic City. Humphrey, Stokely, King, Abernathy, Moses, Fannie, and other MFDP delegates.

SENATOR HUBERT HUMPHREY Alright, a lot of good people have spent a lot of time and energy working this out. The plan is to seat everybody, all sixty-eight of your people, as Honorary Delegates!

FANNIE LOU HAMER "Honorary?"

AARON HENRY What does that mean?

SENATOR HUBERT HUMPHREY It means, Mr. Henry, that you wouldn't vote but you would have *all the other rights and privileges of any other delegate.*

RALPH ABERNATHY No votes!?

Howls of protest.

AARON HENRY The MFDP can accept no less than equal votes at the convention.

BOB MOSES The time has come for Negroes to speak for Negroes; for Negroes to represent Negroes.

SENATOR HUBERT HUMPHREY I have to disagree with you, Bob! If your position is true, then representative democracy is not real and this cannot be a society in which we all live in peace as brothers.

MLK Integration and enfranchisement are not mutually exclusive. This is not what we talked about, Senator.

AARON HENRY After everything we have been through, the MFDP has *earned* the right to be seated.

FANNIE LOU HAMER As full delegates.

SENATOR HUBERT HUMPHREY I don't disagree. In principle. You all know what kind of man I am. I came out in 1948 for civil rights, I've worked all my life for civil rights, and I will be able to do a lot more, a voting rights bill, *if* I'm the Vice President but if we're not able to see reason together here, the President has made it very clear that's not going to happen. (*beat*) And who will he pick instead? Well, it will certainly be someone a lot less sympathetic to the Cause.

FANNIE LOU HAMER Senator Humphrey, you're a good man, and you know what's right. The trouble is, you're afraid to do what you know is right. How can you think your bein' Vice President is more important than 400,000 Black people's lives?

SENATOR HUBERT HUMPHREY Mrs. Hamer, I never said that.

FANNIE LOU HAMER No, sir, but that's what you mean.

STOKELY CARMICHAEL You're tryin' to get the Freedom party to sell out!

SENATOR HUBERT HUMPHREY No, I'm trying to get the most supportive president since Abraham Lincoln re-elected!

LIGHTS down on Pageant Hotel and UP on LBJ/Jenkins. LBJ is wearing pants, socks, t-shirt, and a bathrobe. He looks increasingly haggard. Humphrey moves into their light.

I walked into the Lion's den. I argued fervently, I used all the heartstrings I had, and I made no headway. The least I think they might accept—would be giving them some actual votes. A few votes.

LBJ What did King say?

SENATOR HUBERT HUMPHREY He was mostly quiet.

LBJ After everything I did for him? He shoulda stood up for me! Why didn't somebody stand up for me?

SENATOR HUBERT HUMPHREY I stood up for you, Mr. President.

LBJ Somebody who matters.

SENATOR HUBERT HUMPHREY Well, if you don't think my loyalty is important . . .

LBJ . . . Jesus, you are so thin-skinned. I depend on you, Hubert, you know that. Christ, there's got to be a solution here. OK, maybe we could get one or two of the Mississippi regulars to agree to step aside; they claim they're sick or somethin', so nobody thinks we pressured anybody.

SENATOR HUBERT HUMPHREY Would Eastland go for that?

LBJ Jim has become a tad more helpful since I stepped on his pecker. Alright, you tell 'em they can have *two* voting delegates— we'll call them "at large" delegates—but one of them has to be that white minister of theirs.

SENATOR HUBERT HUMPHREY Reverend Edwin King?

LBJ Yeah, him. That way it's one white man and only one nigra. We'll *integrate* their delegation. Who can argue with that?

SENATOR HUBERT HUMPHREY I'll see what I can do.

LBJ Don't "see what you can do." *Do what I tell you to do.*

Humphrey nods and leaves. LBJ turns to Walter.

We need to light a fire under Hubert. Where is Walter Reuther right now? I need to talk to him.

Walter begins dialing.

WALTER JENKINS Detroit. The UAW is negotiating a new contract with Ford.

LBJ What do you think of Hubert?

WALTER JENKINS (*diplomatically*) I think he's working as hard as he can.

LBJ He's *nice*. Nice is what you call a gal with no tits, no ass, and no personality. Nice is for kissin' babies; there's no place for "nice" in a knife fight.

WALTER JENKINS Mr. Reuther? The President would like a word with you.

SPOT UP on **REUTHER** *on phone in Detroit.*

WALTER REUTHER   Mr. President? What a pleasant surprise. I thought you'd be all busy writing your acceptance speech and . . .

LBJ (*interrupting*)   I know how important your Golden Boy Humphrey is to you and the rest of Organized Labor but if this big delegate war comes off and the South walks out of the Convention he will have no future in the Democratic Party. You hear me? You need to tighten your leash and bring King and the MFDP in line, or by God, Hubert H. Humphrey is never gonna be my Vice President, or anything else!

WALTER REUTHER (*shocked*)   . . . Mr. President . . .

LBJ   When I'm done with him, he won't be able to get elected dog catcher and you'll have nobody in the Senate to carry water for you. You need to get yourself down to Atlantic City and fix this mess and I mean *now!*

LBJ hangs up. SPOT on Reuther out.

WALTER JENKINS (*concerned*)   Are you alright, sir?

LBJ   I do not have the hide of a rhinoceros. People think I have no feelings but they're wrong.

WALTER JENKINS   Yes, sir.

LBJ   You know me, Walter. I have a genuine desire to unite people but my own people in the South are against me, and the North is against me, and the Negroes are against me, and the Press sure doesn't have any damn affection for me.

WALTER JENKINS   It's not fair, sir, not with all you've done.

LBJ   It sure as hell isn't. Year after year, you pour your heart's blood into Public Service, your own kids don't know you, and for what? I could drop dead tomorrow and there wouldn't be ten people who'd shed a tear.

LBJ sits on the bed.

WALTER JENKINS   That's not true, sir.

LBJ   The hell it ain't. People turn on you so fast. When my daddy lost everything, people who'd been glad-handing him treated him like dog shit. Humiliated him to his face in public. And my mother, the way she would freeze him out; that's what killed him. You know what I think it is? People think I want great power but what I want, is great solace; a little love. That's all I want.

WALTER JENKINS   You have that from us, sir. From me.

LBJ smiles at Walter and crawls into bed.

LBJ   I bet poor Marjorie is wonderin' where the hell you are.

Walter turns off a light.

WALTER JENKINS   Oh, she understands.

LBJ   How many kids you got again? Five?

WALTER JENKINS   Six. Two girls and four boys.

LBJ   Right, Catholic. I always wanted to have a son. Don't get me wrong, I love Luci and Lynda, but a man wants a son. I reckon you're as close to that as I've got.

Walter stops and stares at him, deeply touched. He reaches over and removes LBJ's glasses.

WALTER JENKINS   I'll be right next door, sir, if you need me.

Walter leaves. SPOT down on LBJ. SPOT UP on Reuther and King, Hotel, Atlantic City.

MLK   Mr. Reuther? Didn't expect to see you here.

WALTER REUTHER   Neither did I. Had a phone call from the President with a generous helping of the old Texas Twist. You've got to get the MFDP to compromise.

MLK   What the President has offered is a joke; an insult. These people have shed their blood to get here and . . .

WALTER REUTHER   . . . *Your funding is on the line.* Get the MFDP to get on board or there'll be no more Union money for the Movement. Not a single goddamn dime.

MLK   Are you serious?

WALTER REUTHER   Fuck, yes.

MLK   You would sabotage the entire civil rights movement over this?

WALTER REUTHER   No, *you would.* In the great scheme of things, what difference does it really make, Martin? The number of delegates at a convention? Who cares!

MLK   It's wrong.

WALTER REUTHER   Well, you can go home and feel really righteous while all the progress we've made comes to a complete stop, or you can make the sensible play here and see integration become the law of the land. There will be one more offer. A *final* offer. Get your people to accept it, Martin, or take your tin cup and your principles out onto the street and see how far that gets you.

Reuther leaves. SPOT expands to include Humphrey and the rest of the MFDP leadership: Moses, Fannie Lou Hamer, Edwin King, etc.

SENATOR HUBERT HUMPHREY   I'm pleased to say, we've come up with a mighty fine compromise. The MFDP will get two *voting delegates*, Aaron Henry and Edwin King, AND the Democratic Party will adopt a formal rules change to prohibit any segregated delegation in the future.

Stokely steps into the next room, where a TV is playing.

This is a major victory!

FANNIE LOU HAMER   Senator Humphrey, God did not send us to Atlantic City for no two seats when all of us is tired.

AARON HENRY   That's right.

BOB MOSES   This is just like the white plantation boss making all the decisions for his black sharecroppers.

SENATOR HUBERT HUMPHREY   Now, let's just hold on, Bob. You've won your case in the court of public opinion and now you've got your token representation . . .

AARON HENRY   "Token!"

SENATOR HUBERT HUMPHREY   Don't twist my words! What I'm saying is, there is a whole lot at stake here and this is a necessary political compromise.

BOB MOSES   We're not here to bring politics to our morality; we're here to bring morality to our politics.

FANNIE LOU HAMER   Dr. King? What do you think we ought to do?

Everybody looks to MLK—torn between his conscience and political necessity.

MLK   If I were a Mississippi Negro, been through what you've been through, I would vote against it. But the solemn commitment to end discrimination in all future conventions is, as our friend Senator Humphrey suggests, a mighty big victory in which the MFDP could take real pride and as a Negro leader, I'm asking—I want you to take this.

An awkward silence.

EDWIN KING   I don't, uh, feel comfortable being the representative here in place of the grass-roots leadership. Maybe I should step aside, let Mrs. Hamer take my place.

SENATOR HUBERT HUMPHREY   The President is insisting on your presence Edwin because he wants an inter-racial delegation!

EDWIN KING   I'm sure that Mrs. Hamer has to be a part of this.

SENATOR HUBERT HUMPHREY   The President has said that he will not let that illiterate woman speak on the floor of the Democratic convention.

105

RALPH ABERNATHY What kind of racist bullshit is that!

SENATOR HUBERT HUMPHREY (*defensively*) I'm not a racist; that's what the President said! And I'm sure what he meant by that . . .

Stokely, furious, enters the room.

STOKELY CARMICHAEL It's on TV right now! The Credentials Committee is saying that we all agreed to your two delegate plan and they just passed it with a voice vote! *It's over.*

AARON HENRY This whole meeting was a *set-up* just to get us outta the way while you cut your damn deal.

STOKELY CARMICHAEL You're a fucking traitor!

HENRY storms out, followed by Hamer, Abernathy, Stokely, and others, leaving only Humphrey, King, and Moses.

SENATOR HUBERT HUMPHREY (*bewildered and ashamed*) Honestly, Martin, I didn't know about any announcement. This is news to me. I swear it.

Humphrey exits.

BOB MOSES Well done, Doctor King. Solomon himself couldn't have cut that baby in half any cleaner.

MLK "The Moral Arc of the Universe bends towards Justice"; but very slowly.

BOB MOSES I'd say the Moral Arc wasn't much in evidence around here. When we were organizing the MFDP you stood up to Roy Wilkins and told him to his face, "After those three kids were murdered, we have got to take a stand."

MLK When LBJ wins and we get that Voting Rights Bill, this will all be worthwhile.

BOB MOSES You think Goodman and Chaney and Schwerner will feel that way?

Moses walks off. LIGHT SHIFT. LBJ in bed. Walter comes in.

WALTER JENKINS Mr. President? It's Governor Sanders of Georgia.

LBJ Not now.

WALTER JENKINS He says it's urgent.

LBJ sits up and takes the phone. SPOT on **SANDERS**.

LBJ What is it, Carl?

GOVERNOR SANDERS Mr. President, you can't give those people two seats; makes it look like the niggers have taken over the convention!

LBJ For Christ's sake, Carl, it's one Negro and one white minister.

GOVERNOR SANDERS It's the principle of the thing. Me and my delegates might just walk out ourselves and God only knows who will follow us. The whole South might bolt!

LBJ Let's you and me understand somethin' here. "Those people" are Democrats, just like you and me, but those Mississippi good ole boys locked 'em out.

GOVERNOR SANDERS They locked 'em out 'cause they aren't registered to vote!

LBJ *'Cause they won't let 'em register!* Intimidated 'em. Beat 'em. Shot 'em. Lynched 'em . . .

GOVERNOR SANDERS . . . Now you're tarring a lotta people with . . .

LBJ . . . Carl, you and I just can't survive our political modern life with these goddamn fellows down there doing things the old way and eating them nigras for breakfast every morning. They got to quit that.

GOVERNOR SANDERS Mr. President . . .

LBJ . . . No! You listen to me. You need to make up your mind once and for all, just what kinda Christian you are. Are you a once a week fella, or do you hold the Word in your heart? What kind of politician are you? You just out for yourself, or do you wanta make a better life for all the people of Georgia? And what kind of Man are you? You got the balls to do what you know is right, or do you just slink away?

Lady Bird enters, holding the new suit we saw being tailored in the beginning.

What you don't get to do is threaten me. If you want to walk out then do it right now. And if not, then I expect to see your bright and shiny faces wearing your big, "All the way with LBJ" hats tonight when I take the stage!

LBJ slams the phone down and sees Lady Bird.

Go away, Bird, and leave me be.

LBJ curls up in bed.

LADY BIRD JOHNSON   No, Lyndon, I can't do that. I won't.

LBJ   You're just like the rest of 'em. They're all against me. All of 'em.

LADY BIRD JOHNSON   That is so not true. Look at me. *Look at me, Lyndon.*

Something new in her tone of voice makes LBJ sit up.

There are many, many people up there at that convention, in this party, and in this nation who love you, love you dearly. And they are counting on you.

LBJ   I'm gonna resign. Let somebody else deal with it.

LADY BIRD JOHNSON   No, you are not.

LBJ   Yes, I am.

LADY BIRD JOHNSON   *No, you are not going to resign.* When your great-grandmother was hiding under the floorboards while the Comanches were raiding her house, did she flinch? It's just not in your blood. To step down now would be wrong for your country.

Your friends would be frozen in embarrassment and *your enemies would jeer.*

LBJ The bastards would love to see me down.

LADY BIRD JOHNSON That's right, they would. And are you gonna give them that pleasure? I don't think so. That's not the man I married.

Walter runs in, excited.

WALTER JENKINS Governor Sanders was just on TV, the Georgia delegation is not going to walk out of the convention.

LBJ Sanders backed down?

WALTER JENKINS Yes, sir, he did. In fact, the only delegations leaving are Mississippi and Alabama and you pretty much suspected that all along.

LBJ gets up, reinvigorated, the prize fighter responding to the bell.

LADY BIRD JOHNSON It's a great victory, darling!

LBJ The South held?

WALTER JENKINS Yes, sir!

LADY BIRD JOHNSON Yes, they did!

LBJ By God, that's something, innit? Where's my suit?!

LADY BIRD JOHNSON I just had it pressed.

Lady Bird helps LBJ to get dressed. Perhaps on the TB we begin to see images of the excited Delegates and hear the sound of their impatient clapping.

LBJ Walter, tell Humphrey I wanta see him right away, he's gonna be my candidate for Vice-President of the United States! Better have some smellin' salts handy, and a stretcher and an ambulance, he might just keel over! No, no, get Walter Reuther first, we'll give him the good news that his Golden Boy is on board and *then* call Humphrey.

Then call a press conference for the Rose Garden in one hour. Round 'em all up. Tell 'em the big news they've been waiting for is ready to go! Maybe slip an early word first to Katharine Graham at the *Washington Post*. I'll need to talk to Uncle Dick on the phone; I'm sure he had something to do with Carl suddenly growing himself a set of balls and keeping the South in line. And send a written note to Hoover from me thanking him for his service, and contributing to the successful outcome of the convention, etcetera, and, uh no. Hoover. *Nothing in writing.* Just call Hoover and tell him for me. (*to Lady Bird*) How do I look?

LADY BIRD JOHNSON   Magnificent, darlin'!

LBJ and Lady Bird move down into a SPOT just backstage of the Convention Podium, where they are greeted by Humphrey and Muriel.

MURIEL HUMPHREY   Mr. President!

LBJ   Muriel, you look good as gold!

MURIEL HUMPHREY   Thank you, Mr. President! It's a great day!

LADY BIRD JOHNSON   We are so happy for you both; and so proud to have you beside us!

While Lady Bird hugs Muriel, LBJ pulls Humphrey aside.

LBJ   Congratulations, Mr. Almost Vice President!

SENATOR HUBERT HUMPHREY   Thank you, sir.

LBJ   You seem a little down in the mouth.

SENATOR HUBERT HUMPHREY   It just feels—different, than I thought it would.

LBJ   Oh, that. You get over that pretty quick.

*Music blares. LBJ ascends to the podium followed by Humphrey, Lady Bird, and Muriel. A roar of approval from the **DELEGATES**. LBJ inhales their applause. He is on fire—sending the troops into battle.*

I humbly accept your nomination to be the Democratic candidate for President of the United States! In the last few weeks shrill voices have tried to lay claim to the great spirit of the American past, but they long for a past that never was. In their recklessness and their radicalism they have kidnapped the Republican Party and if they win, they will bring this country to the brink of disaster. This is the most important election of your lifetime. The choices couldn't be clearer. Peace or War; Brotherhood or Division; Prosperity or Poverty; a march into a bright future, or a retreat into a dark past. It's all or nothing and every single one of you needs to go out there and fight for every single vote in every part of this great country of ours! God bless you and God bless America!

Everyone on stage begins chanting:

EVERYONE   ALL THE WAY WITH LBJ! ALL THE WAY WITH LBJ! ALL THE WAY WITH LBJ! ALL THE WAY WITH LBJ! ALL THE WAY WITH LBJ!

Cameras flash. Cheers abruptly cut out. New sound emerges—low, threatening—which will hover and build slowly in background until Election Night. LIGHTS SHIFT. TB reads: **40 DAYS TO THE ELECTION.**

LBJ moves into Oval Office—a man on a mission.

LIGHTS UP on Witnesses scattered about the stage. Each interjection is like a hammer blow on LBJ's heart. **[X]** *indicates sound of thunderclap.*

WITNESS #1   Georgia. LBJ down by 5 points!

[X]

WITNESS #3   Mississippi. Goldwater beating Johnson by 60 percent!

[X]

WITNESS #5   South Carolina. LBJ down 6 points!

[X]

WITNESS #2   Louisiana. LBJ down by 8 points!

[X]

LBJ Walter!

Walter runs in with stacks of polls and campaign materials which he puts on the desk. LBJ shuffles through them hungrily.

Change my travel schedule to give me more time in the South, especially Louisiana, and put more money into our TV campaign, they're beatin' the hell out of me. GO!

[X]

Walter runs out as Humphrey runs in. TB reads **37 DAYS TO THE ELECTION.**

Hubert! You see this bullshit *Wall Street Journal* "exposé" about my "corruption"?

SENATOR HUBERT HUMPHREY Definitely planted by Goldwater.

LBJ They're spreadin' rumors I've had another heart attack. I have cancer. I have a drinkin' problem. (*quietly panicked*) He's gettin' on top, Hubert. The son of a bitch is turnin' it around.

SENATOR HUBERT HUMPHREY Mr. President, the polls have you well ahead in most of the country.

LBJ And you believe those lies? *It's a trap.* Goldwater wants to get down into the mud? By God, I can do that. I want you to pull together a special group here in the White House, separate from the campaign, and hit back hard with everything we've got. Don't worry about what it costs; just get it done.

[X]

Humphrey exits. LIGHTS SHIFT.

Ladybird! Walter!

Lady Bird and Walter enter quickly. TB reads: **33 DAYS TO THE ELECTION.**

Congratulations, Bird, you're gonna make history: the first First Lady to campaign on her own! Walter will give you the details of your speakin' tour through the South.

LADYBIRD (*horrified*)   Speak in Public?

LBJ   Unless you'd rather dance for 'em.

LADYBIRD   You know I can't do speeches, Lyndon, I get too nervous.

LBJ   Well, it's high time you learned! And you're gonna take Lynda and Luci with you. It's all hands on deck. Go on, get packed!

[X]
Lady Bird and Walter run out. LIGHTS SHIFT. TB reads: **30 DAYS TO THE ELECTION.** *SPOT on Witnesses.*

WITNESSES   GEORGIA!

WITNESS #1   LBJ now down by 7 points and falling fast!

[X]

WITNESSES   MISSISSIPPI!

WITNESS #3   Goldwater beating Johnson by 70 percent!

[X]

LBJ   Walter!

WITNESSES   FLORIDA!

WITNESS #4   Goldwater beating LBJ by two points!

[X]

WITNESSES   SOUTH CAROLINA!

WITNESS #5   LBJ down 10 points!

[X]

LBJ   WALTER!

113

[X]

LBJ   Walter?

LIGHTS SHIFT. Hoover enters, very worried.

J. EDGAR HOOVER   Arrested in the Men's bathroom of the YMCA by the Washington, D.C., Vice Squad.

A drunk, disheveled, and terrified Walter is frog-marched through the Oval Office in handcuffs by two VICE SQUAD OFFICERS to a position SR. Tight SPOT on Walter.

TB reads: **27 DAYS TO THE ELECTION.**

LBJ (*incredulous*)   Walter was arrested?

J. EDGAR HOOVER   Yes, sir. The other man arrested with him was a retired Staff Sergeant in the Army.

LBJ   No. Gotta be some kind of mistake.

J. EDGAR HOOVER   No, sir. (*hesitant*) Apparently, he was arrested, under similar circumstances, five years ago.

Simultaneously, Walter's mug-shot is photographed: Left Profile, Right Profile, Center Front.

LBJ (*furious*)   Why didn't I know that?

J. EDGAR HOOVER   None of us knew.

LBJ   Sounds like some kind of a Republican dirty trick set-up to me.

Camera flash.

J. EDGAR HOOVER   We're investigating that angle but it's hard to see how this could have been arranged.

Camera flash.

LBJ   But Goldwater will use it. You know the son of a bitch will use it. This close to the election? This could be the whole ball of wax!

114

Camera flash.

J. EDGAR HOOVER   There doesn't appear to be any Security compromise at all.

LBJ   There damn well better not be. *Your people* were supposed to vet him. You said they did. I have that in writing with your goddamn signature on it.

J. EDGAR HOOVER *(panicked)*   Some things you can't predict.

LBJ   That's your job, Jay!

J. EDGAR HOOVER   I will take care of this, Mr. President!

In response to a command by the Vice Squad Officers, Walter begins to remove his clothes until he is in only his underwear.

LBJ   Why doesn't that make me feel better? Christ on a cross. Get me Walter's Air Force Reserve records. Goldwater was his Commanding Officer and with any luck, he signed off on his Fitness Evaluations. We get a hold of those and Goldwater won't be able to say shit. Walter will have to resign immediately. See that his Doctor issues a statement: nervous breakdown, workin' too hard and just snapped. Then get him into the psych ward at Walter Reed. No visitors. No incomin' phone calls. *Nothing.*

J. EDGAR HOOVER   I can't just lock him up . . .

LBJ   CLEAN UP YOUR MESS! I worked with that man for twenty-five years. Not a clue. *(a threat)* How do you know when somebody's that way?

J. EDGAR HOOVER   Well, well, there are certain signs; mannerisms. The way a man—dresses or combs his hair. Or walks kind of funny.

LBJ   News to me. I'm not questioning you; *I'm sure you'd know*—in your line of work, I mean. Take care of this.

Hoover leaves. Vice Squad Officers leave. LIGHT SHIFT. Lady Bird enters.

LADY BIRD JOHNSON   Marjorie is just beside herself; can't believe it's true! I can't believe it's true. I'm going to make a public statement of support.

LBJ   No! Absolutely not. The First Lady can't be involved in this. None of us can be involved.

LADY BIRD JOHNSON   He's distraught, Lyndon. He might injure himself!

A **NURSE** *enters and brusquely helps Walter into a hospital gown.*

LBJ   That is not my problem.

LADY BIRD JOHNSON (*shocked*)   *He is our friend!*

LBJ   He was our friend and then he stabbed me in the back!

LADY BIRD JOHNSON   Are we never gonna see him again?

LBJ   You think I like this? Goldwater is killin' me in the polls! *I loved Walter like a . . .*

Walter exits SR.

. . . I am holdin' this campaign together with bailin' wire and spit and if you are not with me, then you are against me!

LADY BIRD JOHNSON (*furious*)   I'm not against you, Lyndon; I have speeches to make.

[X]

Lady Bird exits SL. LIGHTS SHIFT. TB: **14 DAYS TO THE ELECTION.** **TELEVISION ANNOUNCER** *enters.*

TELEVISION ANNOUNCER   And in what is sure to be a very controversial decision, the winner of this year's Nobel Prize for Peace is Dr. Martin Luther King!

Cheers. TB: **NOBEL PRIZE CEREMONY. OSLO, NORWAY.** *SPOT on King and Coretta as they make their way to DSR where the* **KING OF NORWAY** *is waiting. Hoover and Deloach stand CS in*

116

their own SPOT watching in disgust. TB: **FBI HEADQUARTERS, WASHINGTON, D.C.**

J. EDGAR HOOVER   I'm supposed to have psychic abilities to protect the President from deviants like Jenkins but when it comes to King, when it comes to King apparently no warning is strong enough! That's it. Get me the goddamn sex tapes of King with those women.

LIGHTS UP CS as LBJ crosses to meet Humphrey at the "backstage area" of an auditorium in New Orleans. LBJ is anxious and angry. TB: **NEW ORLEANS. DEMOCRATIC CAMPAIGN RALLY. 12 DAYS TO THE ELECTION.** *The audience sounds hostile; clapping and jeering.*

SENATOR HUBERT HUMPHREY   I don't understand why you're ignoring Dr. King. Surely a public acknowledgement from the White House is important?

LBJ   King knows where I stand; I don't need to get on the goddamn rooftops and shout it out, especially not here in New Orleans. Goldwater's now up twenty-two points in Louisiana!

LBJ nervously studies his speech. King and Coretta have reached the Dais and are waving to the audience.

CORETTA KING (*angry*)   I cannot believe the President is ignoring you like this.

MLK   We might have to do something different to get his attention.

Throughout the following, the King of Norway will ceremoniously shake hands with the Kings, and then formally drape the Nobel Medal around MLK's neck. Pictures are taken.

SENATOR HUBERT HUMPHREY   It's just there are ugly rumors that Hoover has ratcheted up his campaign against King.

LBJ   I'm not gonna get into a pissin' contest with Hoover just days before the election.

Chants of "Goldwater" surge in volume.

117

What the hell is wrong with those people; this is a *Democratic* rally for Christ's sake. Where's the Governor?

SENATOR HUBERT HUMPHREY (*bitter*)   He left an hour ago; suddenly called, "out of town."

LBJ (*coldly furious*)   Cowardly son of a bitch. You hear what they did to Lady Bird this mornin' in South Carolina? Burned a cross in front of her and called her a "communist" and a "nigger-lover." I have had enough of this shit. (*yells at* **ANNOUNCER**) Let's get a move on!

KING OF NORWAY   Ladies and Gentlemen, may I present the winner of the Nobel Prize for Peace, DR. MARTIN LUTHER KING!

MLK moves DSR to a podium to the sound of enthusiastic applause.

NEW ORLEANS ANNOUNCER   And now, let's give a warm New Orleans welcome to the PRESIDENT OF THE UNITED STATES!

LBJ "enters" DC to a chorus of "Boos."

LBJ   Alright you've had your say, now I'm gonna have mine!

More Boos. LBJ stares back—a moment of decision. He crumples up his prepared speech.

MLK   I accept this award on behalf of a Civil Rights Movement which is moving with determination to establish a reign of freedom and a rule of justice.

LBJ   My fellow Southerners—*my fellow Southerners.* Like you, I grieve for the condition of our beloved South.

The audience quiets as LBJ lowers his voice and makes an appeal to their conscience direct from his heart.

MLK   Only yesterday in Alabama, our children, crying out for brotherhood, were answered with fire hoses, dogs, and even death.

LBJ Like you, I have watched with sadness and quiet fury as self-serving politicians have divided and conquered us with the poisonous lie of racial hatred.

MLK Only yesterday in Mississippi, young people seeking the right to vote were brutalized and murdered.

LBJ For over a hundred years, nobody's dared to speak the truth. All we ever hear at election time is: "NIGGER! NIGGER! NIGGER!"

MLK I refuse to believe that we are so tragically bound to the starless midnight of racism . . .

LBJ Well, not anymore. I am not gonna let them build up the hate.

MLK . . . that the bright daybreak of brotherhood can never become a reality.

LBJ I am not gonna let them trick my people by appealin' to their prejudice.

MLK I still believe in the promise of America.

LBJ Whatever your views are, we have a Constitution.

MLK I still believe that we all can have dignity, equality, and freedom.

LBJ Whatever your views are, we have a new law of the land.

MLK I still believe . . .

LBJ A civil rights law.

MLK . . . That we shall overcome.

LBJ And you can vote for me or vote against me but I signed it, and by God, I am going to enforce it because it is the right thing to do *and high time we did it!*

Sounds of standing ovation in both Oslo and New Orleans.

MLK exits. LBJ alone on stage, looks at the TB. Titles: **NOVEMBER 3, 1964! ELECTION NIGHT!** *Multiple streaming IMAGES* *showing election returns surging in state by state, along with IMAGES of intense, worried* **VOTERS** *and* **STAFFERS**, *eventually morphing into a giant ELECTORAL MAP starkly revealing LBJ'S landslide victory.*

The stage is suddenly flooded with ecstatic LBJ **SUPPORTERS**, *waving flags. Confetti falls as they surround LBJ, chanting, "ALL THE WAY WITH LBJ! ALL THE WAY WITH LBJ!" Red, White and Blue silk banners fall from the sky. Sounds of fireworks and cheering crowds. Patriotic bunting drapes the stage.*

Lady Bird pulls LBJ slightly away. As she does so, the supporters move US.

LADY BIRD JOHNSON   *Sixteen million votes!* Don't tell me this country doesn't love you, darlin'!

Lady Bird hugs LBJ. He smiles but seems withdrawn. From across the room . . .

PARTY GOER   BIRD!

LADY BIRD JOHNSON (*to LBJ*)   Be right back!

Lady Bird runs over and hugs her friend as McNamara approaches LBJ from the other side, carrying a distinctive red folder.

ROBERT MCNAMARA   Congratulations, Mr. President. And my apologies.

McNamara hands the red folder to LBJ.

MCNAMARA (*quietly*)   From our Ambassador in Saigon.

As LBJ opens the folder and scans the briefing paper, simultaneously a SPOT comes up on MLK and FRIENDS at home watching the election on TV and celebrating. A doorbell rings.

MLK   Coretta! Can you get that?!

Coretta enters SR carrying a cardboard box.

CORETTA KING   It's for you, Martin! You want me to open it?!

MLK Yeah, sure!

A triumphant Humphrey approaches LBJ from the other side opposite McNamara. McNamara drifts discreetly US. LBJ closes the folder and holds it down, away from Humphrey.

VICE-PRESIDENT HUMPHREY CONGRATULATIONS, MR. PRESIDENT; A HISTORIC VICTORY! Sixty-one percent of the popular vote. We picked up forty-eight House seats and even two seats in the Senate!

LBJ Yeah, Bobby won New York.

VICE-PRESIDENT HUMPHREY Bobby Kennedy is no challenge! He never was.

LBJ (*distracted*) Uh-huh.

MLK (*re: the box*) What was it?

Coretta now has the box open and lifts out a tape and holds it up.

CORETTA KING Just a buncha tapes!

VICE-PRESIDENT HUMPHREY Hell, Goldwater only carried six states!

MLK I'll be there in a minute!

Coretta pulls out a tape player and headphones. She puts on the headphones and listens to the tape recorder, a look of horror growing on her face.

LBJ (*quiet; pained*) Count the votes, Hubert. He won five *Southern* states, including Georgia. Hell, Georgia has never voted Republican, not even during Reconstruction. Time was, we could win the South with Farm support and programs for poor people but not this time, no, this time they voted against their own interests so they could wave the bloody flag *and Goldwater was crazy.* Wait 'till the Party of Lincoln gets some slick, sweet-smiling candidate, somebody a little more presentable. Count the goddamn votes. Get me a drink.

121

Humphrey exits. McNamara moves to LBJ.

ROBERT MCNAMARA What would you like us to do, sir?

LBJ hands the red folder back.

LBJ I need to think on it.

McNamara nods and moves DSR where he waits and watches, clutching the red folder.

Abernathy puts an arm around MLK as they stare at the TV news.

RALPH ABERNATHY *(re: the TV)* Look. Look! "Ninety-six percent of the Negro vote to Johnson." They owe us big time, Martin. Now they'll give us that Voting Rights Bill!

MLK LBJ's not gonna *give* us anything; we have to take it. We're gonna start a new campaign. Right away. In Alabama.

SPOT comes up on Wallace (cigar in hand) and Lurleen DSL watching the celebration on TV.

LURLEEN WALLACE *(re: the TV results)* I'm so sorry, George. I guess that's it, huh?

GOVERNOR GEORGE WALLACE That's what?

Coretta approaches MLK, tape recorder and headphones in hand.

CORETTA KING Martin? What have you done?

MLK What is it, baby?

LURLEEN WALLACE I guess it's over.

Coretta hands MLK the headphones and moves away while MLK listens to the tape.

Lady Bird finds LBJ.

LADY BIRD JOHNSON I'm so glad it's over, aren't you?

LBJ smiles warmly at Lady Bird and wraps an arm around her.

GOVERNOR GEORGE WALLACE   Hell, Lurleen, ain't nothin' over.

LBJ   Over?

GOVERNOR GEORGE WALLACE/LBJ   *It's just gettin' started.*

LADY BIRD JOHNSON   What are you doing in here, standing by yourself? Everybody's waitin' on you!

Lady Bird gently tries to pull LBJ towards the party. Suddenly, LBJ pulls Lady Bird into him and kisses her passionately. A moment. LBJ breaks the kiss. Lady Bird is surprised; thrilled.

Come join the party, darling. *Your* Party.

LBJ   In a minute.

Lady Bird moves US. LIGHTS FADE DOWN to single SPOT on LBJ.

(*to audience*) You're goddamn right it's my Party and I had to drag it into the light kickin' and screamin' every inch of the way. Did it make you feel a little squeamish? Did you have to look away sometimes? 'Cause this is how new things are born. Bird and I lost three babies 'fore we had Lynda. I remember the moment when they finally let me into the room to see my first live child and there on the floor you could still see the footprints of the doctors in my wife's blood and I thought, yeah, this is familiar. *I know this.*

There is a burst of laughter and noise and the **CROWD** *starts singing, "Happy Days Are Here Again!"*

(*to audience*) But right now we're gonna party like there's no tomorrow 'cause there's no feeling in the world half as good as winning! But the sun *will* come up and the knives will come out and all these smiling faces will be watchin' me, watchin' me, waitin' for that one, first moment of weakness, and then they will gut me like a deer.

LIGHTS rise to include ALL as everyone else on stage finishes singing and is now staring at LBJ.

REST OF COMPANY "HA-PPY. DAYS. ARE. HERE. A-GAIN!"

Everyone but Lady Bird/LBJ freeze. Lady Bird shouts to LBJ from across the stage.

LADY BIRD JOHNSON You OK, honey?!

LBJ answers Lady Bird but his eyes never leave the audience.

LBJ I'm fine, Bird. I'm great. *(fierce; triumphant)* HELL, I'M PRESIDENT!

LBJ stares defiantly at the Audience as the Lights BLACKOUT.

END OF PLAY.